SWEATERS

SWEATERS

**28 Contemporary
Designs
in the
Norwegian
Tradition**

*LISE KOLSTAD
&
TONE TAKLE*

English Adaptation by
Robin Orm Hansen

INTERWEAVE
PRESS

ABBREVIATIONS

dec	decrease
inc	increase
k	knit
kb	knit in back of stitch
p	purl
pb	purl in back of stitch
rnd	round
st	stitch
dp	double pointed
cir	circular
tog	together
yd/lb	yards per pound
oz	ounces

English translation: Robin Orm Hansen
Photography: Johannes Bøe
Knitting illustrations: Lise Kolstad
Cover design: Susan Wasinger/Signorella Graphic Arts
Production: Marc McCoy Owens

Interweave Press
201 East Fourth Street
Loveland, Colorado 80537

ISBN 0-934026-76-9

Library of Congress Cataloging-in-Publication Data:

Kolstad, Lise.
   [Norske strikkebok. English]
   Sweaters: 28 contemporary designs in the Norwegian tradition /
Lise Kolstad and Tone Takle; English adaptation by Robin Orm Hansen;
[photography, Johannes Bøe; knitting illustrations, Lise Kolstad].
      p.   cm.
   Translation of: Norske strikkebok.
   Includes index.
   ISBN 0-934026-76-9: $16.95
   1. Knitting—Norway—Patterns.   2. Sweaters—Norway.   I. Takle, Tone.
II. Title
   TT825.K671313   1992
   746.9'2—dc20   92-14116
                                          CIP

First printing: 8M:692:CC—Hong Kong

CONTENTS

Foreword

In Norway, knitting tradition and skills have survived as much by being passed from one generation to the next as by being taught to children in the public schools. Knitting here is a living folk culture! We learned to knit from our grandmothers, just as they must have learned from their own grandmothers. We have grown up within a tradition.

What is included in this tradition? Daring, originality, and sophistication characterize what we have seen in museums and in books. "Tradition" in Norway has never meant copying exactly what went before but creating something new as an extension of what others have made. Every knitter has added something of herself and her own taste to the garments she has knitted. Tradition has meant interpreting contemporary fashions in local materials and techniques.

Following this custom, we have adapted today's fashions in the basic designs for this book. But we have tried to understand how the earlier pattern motifs were formulated, how they were used together, and how our ancestors used colors. There is much to learn from earlier generations.

We have been inspired by Norwegian folk art, popular temperament, landscape, and our own imaginations. The patterns we give you can be knitted as they are or used as inspiration to put patterns and colors together in your own way. In the back of the book, you will find directions for the basic designs we have used as well as tips and ideas for creating your own sweater.

Tone Takle and Lise Kolstad

BASIC INFORMATION

If the sweaters you make based on this book are to be excellent, there are a few things you *must* do; on many other points, you may depart from our instructions.

COLORS: Use whatever colors you wish. Find out how exciting it is to put different colors together. Notice the colors of something you like, the color play in woods or clouds, in fabrics, gift wraps, paintings, stones, flowers, autumn leaves, fish, and shells. You can find color inspiration everywhere.

CHARTED PATTERNS: This book contains at least 50 band and motif patterns never before published; use them any way you like. If you plan to combine charted patterns from two different garments, however, please read "A Sweater Is Born" (page 84) to learn how to arrange patterns on a garment. If you use the same charted pattern we used for a given sweater, note the arrows showing where you should begin for each size.

SIZE: Our designs fit loosely. On page 87 you will find a table with approximate measurements for 12 common sizes. Save yourself unpleasant surprises when the sweater is finished by measuring the person who is going to wear the sweater before you choose a size and start to knit.

KNITTING NEEDLES AND GAUGE: If the directions specify two needle sizes, you will usually need double-pointed needles for the sleeves and 24-inch circular needles for the body in both sizes specified. (The smaller size needles are used for the ribbing.) When only one needle size is called for, you will need both 24-inch circular and double-pointed needles.

It is important to knit at exactly the gauge given in the directions. If you don't, the garment may turn out much too big, as we have based our designs on a fairly tight gauge. Make a test swatch in the yarn and color pattern that you expect to use, and experiment with different needle sizes to match our stitch count exactly. If your swatch has too few stitches per inch, try smaller needles than those suggested. We, too, have made the mistake of starting on a large garment without making a test swatch first. In her attic, Tone has a big bag of misbegotten knitting projects made without checking the gauge first. It's irritating to put weeks of work into a project only to have it turn out badly, the more so if it's because you didn't spend 30 minutes making a test swatch of the pattern.

THE INSTRUCTIONS: Read through the entire pattern before you start to knit. Many of the techniques are described in more detail in "Knitting Techniques" (page 9).

BASIC INSTRUCTIONS: Use the basic instructions in "A Sweater Is Born" (page 84) as a starting point for garments from your own imagination. Pick up ideas from the charted patterns and sweater shapes in the book, or design your own.

YARN: All garments in this book were knitted in Rauma brand wool yarn, virgin wool yarn that carries the Woolmark guarantee. Rauma Finullgarn (about 1600 yd/lb) comes in more than 100 colors, and Rauma Strikkegarn (about 1000 yd/lb) also has a rich palette. Both are fairly hard spun. Finullgarn corresponds in size to American sport-weight yarn, and Strikkegarn is equivalent to a light worsted-weight yarn, although both are much more dense than their American counterparts. Rauma yarn types and color numbers are given in the instructions. There is also a generic yarn description so that you can substitute other brands; knit a swatch to find what size needles to use to get the gauge called for in the pattern you choose. Use cotton or other fibers if you wish; as long as your stitch and row counts are the same as those given in the pattern, the sweater will match the intended measurements.

KNITTING
TECHNIQUES

CASTING ON: *Method 1:* The most common method of casting on is the long-tail cast-on taught in Norwegian public schools. With about a 3-foot tail (for a test swatch) make a slipknot loop (detail of figure 1) and put it over the knitting needle. Put the tail end over the thumb of your left hand and the long end around your left index finger so that the loop on the needle lies between the left thumb and index finger. Anchor both ends with the other fingers of your left hand, as shown in figure 1. With the needle in your right hand, *bring the point forward into the loop that has formed around the thumb, then catch (from the right side) the strand on the left side of the index finger and pull it back through the thumb loop. Let the loop slide off your left thumb (figure 2). As you lift the tail end with the back of your left thumb (figure 3), pull up fairly tightly.** Repeat from * to ** until you have as many stitches as you need.

To figure how long a tail you will need for a given project, measure from the tip of your index finger to your wrist. This length corresponds to about 10 stitches. Measure this length repeatedly while counting by tens until you have enough yarn for the number of stitches you need.

Method 2: If you want a more elastic edge, as for a cap, cast on this way: place a slipknot over the knitting needle. Knit into the slipknot with another needle and place the new stitch onto the first needle beside the slipknot (the first stitch). Knit between the two stitches to form the third. Continue knitting between the last two stitches and slipping the new stitch onto the needle until you have enough stitches.

TO INCREASE (inc): Between stitches is a little bar of yarn. Knit a stitch into

1. Long-tail cast-on: Make a slip knot around the needle, hold the yarn as shown, and take the needle up through the thumb loop, around the yarn on the left side of the index finger, and back through the thumb loop.

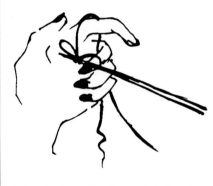

2. Let the loop slip off your left thumb.

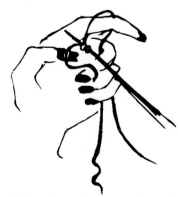

3. Pull up the stitch as you pick up the tail again onto your left thumb.

this crossbar (twisting the stitch as you knit). When the directions say to increase two stitches at the seamline of the sleeve, it looks best if the increases are separated by one or two stitches.

TO DECREASE (dec): *Method 1:* To decrease one stitch, for example at the top of a cap, simply knit two stitches together (k2tog). This decrease causes the visible stitch to lean to the right. You can also use this decrease on raglan shoulders.

Method 2: You can also decrease by slipping a stitch, as if to knit, to the right needle, slipping the next stitch as if to knit, and inserting the left needle into those two stitches and knitting them off as one (ssk). The visible stitch will lean to the left. Experiment to see where you like this type of decrease. If you have two decreases together, separated by one or two stitches, you might want to use this method for the first decrease and k2tog for the second one.

TO BIND OFF: To bind off all stitches, as at the top of a sleeve, knit the first two stitches *loosely,* and slip the first over the second. Knit the third stitch, and slip the second over the third, and so forth. Continue until there is only one stitch left. Break the yarn leaving a short tail, and pull the tail through the last stitch.

TWISTED RIB (k1b, p1b): Some sweaters call for a tight, twisted ribbing. Although this ribbing is made by alternating knit and purl stitches, just as for regular ribbing, the knits and purls are made differently. *Twisted knit (k1b):* Every stitch you knit is essentially a loop hanging on a needle. When you knit a stitch, you pull a new loop through the one already hanging there by inserting the needle through the front side of the loop, front to back. Putting the needle through the back side of the loop, back to front, will produce a twisted knit stitch.

Twisted purl (p1b): With the working yarn in front of the work, put the needle through the back side of the loop, from back to front, and purl, as shown in the drawings on page 10.

Twisted purl: Insert the right needle into the stitch from behind, then follow the arrow with the needle point.

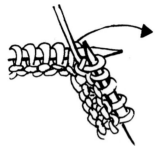

Slip the stitch off the left needle.

KNITTING CHARTED PATTERNS:

In pattern charts, the background color is usually indicated by an empty square, while the pattern colors are shown by a black circle or other symbol in the square.

The word "motif" in a pattern description is the smallest complete unit in a band of pattern. Usually a motif is repeated many times, either widthwise or lengthwise, to create a pattern.

Sometimes the number of stitches in the motif won't fit evenly into the number of stitches across the garment. In that case, we like to center the pattern on the sweater and "cut" the edges of the pattern at the sides of the garment (where the side seams would be if you were to knit back and forth). To give a finished look to the incomplete pattern at the sides, work one or more stitches (called "seam" stitches) in the darkest color used in each round of the pattern. The "seam" stitches will resemble a seam. On the sleeve, it looks attractive to use one or more "seam" stitches where the underarm seam would be, and to increase on each side of these stitches.

WORKING IN LOOSE ENDS:

When the project is finished, thread the tails of yarn on a blunt, large-eye yarn needle and weave them into the back of the fabric. Or weave in loose ends as you knit; if you knit with the yarn over your left finger, place the strand to be woven in closer to the knuckle of your left index finger, then knit alternately over and under this strand. After you've done this five or six times, the strand will be well fastened down. Give a little widthwise pull in that row of stitches before you trim the end. If you knit with the yarn in your right hand, weave in by giving the two yarns a half-twist between stitches. By reversing the direction of this twist each time, you can avoid tangles between the two balls of yarn.

You can use this technique when knitting color patterns with more than seven consecutive stitches in the same color to avoid long loose loops of yarn on the back of your work.

DUPLICATE STITCH:

Embroidered on after the knitting is completed, a duplicate stitche looks exactly like a knit stitch: a little V at the bottom and wrapped around the base of the stitch above.

Duplicate stitches provide many decorative possibilities not afforded by ordinary two-colored knitting. Use them to "knit" cross-stitch charts or to embroider isolated motifs on knitted garments. You can use duplicate stitch within a motif for the least used color when there are more than two colors in a round or when there is a great widthwise distance between single stitches of one color.

After anchoring the end of the yarn on the back side of the work, bring the needle out at the base of the stitch you are overlapping, take it around the back of the stitch above, then push it back through the fabric at the base again.

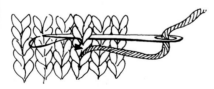

Duplicate stitch: Bring the needle out at the base of the stitch you are overlapping, take it around the back of the stitch above, then push it back through the fabric at the base again.

To reduce bulk, it's wise to embroider duplicate stitch in a somewhat lighter weight yarn than the one you have knitted with, particularly if the embroidery is extensive.

BUTTONHOLES:

Buttonholes can be made several ways. The most common is to bind off a few stitches in one row and cast on the same number in the next row above the bind-off.

You can also knit the stitches for the buttonhole in a scrap of a contrasting yarn. When the knitting is finished, pick out the contrasting yarn and, with a yarn needle, run a strand of matching yarn twice around the hole through the freed stitches and bottom loops. Then sew buttonhole stitch all the way around the buttonhole.

NECK OPENING:

On many patterns, we tell you to bind off for the front and back neck openings but continue to knit in pattern until the body of the sweater has reached its full length. After binding off the front neck stitches, work interrupted rounds (that is, knit across and purl back) across the remaining stitches while maintaining the color pattern until it's time to bind off for the back neck. When the back neck has been bound off, the stitches for the two shoulders will each have to be worked in interrupted rounds until the sweater has reached its total length.

An alternative approach that will allow you to continue knitting circularly is to make a "steek", a narrow section of waste stitches which you will cut through when knitting is completed. To make a steek, bind off the specified number of neck stitches where you want the front opening to be and, in the next round, cast on three new stitches over the bound-off stitches. On each subsequent round, purl these three stitches (the steek) with all strands used in that round so that the area is quite firm. Work the same process for the back neck opening. When the body portion is finished, machine stay-stitch a double seam along each side of the line of purl stitches and cut the two sides apart. This technique can be used wherever you have an opening (center front, front neck, back neck) but prefer to knit circularly.

After the neck opening is complete, pick up and knit an appropriate number of stitches around it and work either ribbing or a facing as indicated in the pattern.

FACINGS & HEMS: Hems and facings are often used to edge garments at the bottom and wrists, as well as at the tops of the sleeves and at the neck. Don't use a facing at the sleeve top if you are using a heavy yarn; it will be too bulky. Begin a sleeve facing with one round of purl so that the facing will spread out nicely and to give you a round to sew into when attaching the sleeve to the body. To purl an entire round, you can simply turn your work inside out and knit plain around. Then turn it right side out again and continue knitting to make the facing.

To face square necks, you must increase one stitch in each corner in every round to make the facing lie flat when turned to the inside of the garment. For a square outside corner, such as the lower front corner of a jacket, you must do the opposite, decreasing a stitch at the corner in every round to make the facing lie flat when turned to the inside of the garment.

FINISHING: On most of the designs, the body and sleeves are knitted separately in the round, then the center front (for cardigans) and armholes are cut into the body, and the sleeves sewn in.

To position the sleeves in the body, carefully baste the location of the side seams on the body, from the shoulder down, if they are not already clearly marked by your color knitting or "seam" stitches. Smooth the body out on a flat surface, lay the sleeve in position at the top of the body, and measure how far down the "seam" the top (armhole) of the sleeve extends. Mark this point with a pin or a basting stitch. With a tiny straight stitch, machine sew along the center of a stitch or between two lines of stitches on one side of the "seam" line to the point marked as the bottom of the armhole. Turn, sew across one knit stitch, then sew back to the top on the other side of the "seam" line. Make another line of straight machine stitches just outside the first, on the same line of knit stitches. Cut between the first two lines of machine stitching. Repeat for the other sleeve. If your sweater is designed

to be a cardigan, machine stitch and cut open the center front in the same way. Turn the body inside out and stitch or knit the shoulders together as described below.

SHOULDER SEAMS: *To sew shoulders together:* If the shoulder edges were bound off, sew the front and back shoulders, right sides together, by hand using a running stitch to tack back and forth between the two. Stitch just inside the bind-off round. *To knit shoulders together:* For a firm seam, knit the front and back shoulder edges together, binding both off at the same time: with the two pieces to be attached side by side on two needles, either right or wrong side out, push a third needle into the first stitch of both needles, then knit both stitches off together loosely. Repeat, then slip the first stitch over the second, and so forth, until only one stitch remains on the right needle. Break the yarn and pull the end through this stitch. Knitting seams together is commonly done from the purl side in Norway, and from the knit side in the British Isles.

ATTACHING SLEEVES: With right sides together, set the sleeve into the armhole. Use a running stitch to tack back and forth between the sleeve and body: on the sleeve, stitch into the round below the purl round or just inside the bind-off round if there is no facing. On the body, sew into the horizontals of the stitches just inside the machine-stitched lines. Draw the stitches up firmly as you go and the facing or seam allowance will automatically turn to the inside. If there is a facing on the top of the sleeve, smooth it over to cover the seam just sewn and stitch it in place by hand.

FINAL DETAILS: Tack down any other hems or facings. With multi-ply yarn, you may wish to remove one ply to reduce bulk in these joinings. Finish the neck opening as described in your pattern. Weave in any loose tails and carefully steam the entire garment under a damp cloth. Some people feel

that knitted garments should never be steamed; this is really a matter of preference.

Numerous books have been published on knitting techniques. The subject is extensive: there are many ways to cast on, bind off, increase and decrease. We have here dealt only with what you will need to knit the garments in this book.

IN THE NORWEGIAN TRADITION

The themes in this chapter are drawn from Norwegian folk art. We've looked at the use of color and ornamentation of rosemaling, peasant dress, wood carving, wrought iron, tapestries, and old pieces of knitting and embroidery.

It is exciting to see how boldly people expressed themselves in the folk art traditions, putting together colors and patterns that are sharply dissimilar or working cleverly with very few colors.

GREEN-SLEEVES PULLOVER

If this pullover had been only red and yellow, the colors would have seemed strident, but adding a closely related background color on the sleeves and part of the body gives it a more subdued effect. So does the change in motif size; the sleeves and yoke have small elements of the large pattern on the body. Of course, nothing should keep you from knitting the sweater in more tranquil colors. You could try gray-blue, olive green, and rust or barn red, all colors with a long tradition in Norwegian culture.

YARN: Worsted-weight wool at about 1000 yd/lb. The sweater shown is knit in Rauma Strikkegarn in the colors listed below.

CHART: page 97.

SIZES: To fit adult sizes S (M, L, XL, XXL). See page 87 for approximate measurements.

COLORS: 4 (4, 4, 6, 6) oz of Dark Brown (color #110); 2 (2, 2, 4, 4) oz of Honey (color #146); 11 (11, 13, 15, 15) oz of Yellow (color #131); 15 (15, 16, 18, 18) oz of Red (color #144); 8 (8, 9, 11, 11) oz of Green (color #198).

GAUGE: 24 sts and 28 rnds = 4 × 4 inches.

SUGGESTED NEEDLE SIZES: Size 3 dp and 24-inch cir needles for sleeves and body. Size 2 dp needles for neck ribbing. Make a sample swatch on size 3 needles following one of the charts to check your gauge, and change needle sizes if necessary to get the proper gauge.

SLEEVE: With Dark Brown yarn, cast on 44 (46, 48, 52, 54) sts on dp needles. Join and work twisted ribbing (k1b, p1b) for 2 (2, 2¼, 2¼, 2½) inches. In the next rnd, change to stockinette st and increase 15 (19, 17, 19, 25) sts evenly spaced for a total of 59 (65, 65, 71, 79) sts. As you work the charts, knit the first and last st of each rnd in the darkest color in that rnd to mark the underarm "seam". The charts show where to begin the pattern after the "seam" sts. At the same time, inc 1 st on each side of the "seam" sts every third (third, second, second, second) rnd. Work the color pattern as follows: work Chart 1 in Dark Brown background and Yellow pattern. Knit 3 rnds in Honey, work Chart 2 in Red pattern and Yellow background, then repeat Chart 3 with Green background and Red pattern until there are 137 (151, 163, 181, 187) sts. Continue repeating Chart 3 until the sleeve measures 19 (18½, 18, 17¾, 17½) inches or desired length above the ribbing. With Green yarn, k 3 rnds, p 1 rnd, and k 7 rnds for the sleeve facing. Bind off. Make another sleeve.

BODY: Cast on 254 (270, 290, 318, 342) sts in Dark Brown. Join and work a twisted rib (k1b, p1b) for 2¾ (2¾, 3, 3¼, 3½) inches. Always k the first 2 and center 2 sts of each rnd in the darkest color in that rnd to mark the side "seams". The chart shows where you should begin in the pattern after knitting the 2 "seam" sts. Work Chart 4 once with Dark Brown pattern and Honey background. Then work Chart 5 with Red pattern and Yellow background until the body measures 21¼ (20¾, 21¼, 21½, 22) inches above the ribbing. Knit 3 rnds in Honey. Begin Chart 3 in Red pattern and Green background until the body measures 21¼ (21¾, 22½, 23, 23½) inches above the ribbing or the desired length to neckline. Bind off the center 15 (15, 15, 15, 17) sts in front for the neck opening. Working back and forth in stockinette st, bind off 4 sts at side of neck opening at beginning of next 2 rows. Knit 1 row even, then in the next 2 rows bind off 4 sts at each side as above. Purl 1 row even, then bind off 3 sts each side. There will be 217 (233, 253, 281, 303) sts remaining. Work ¾ inch in pattern, then bind off the center 25 (25, 25, 25, 27) sts in back for the neck opening. Working the 2 shoulders separately, bind off 3 sts at the back neck opening twice while continuing the pattern. There will be 90 (98, 108, 122, 132) sts on each shoulder. Continue knitting pattern for ½ inch above the back neck opening. Bind off all sts.

FINISHING: Stay-stitch and cut the armholes, sew the shoulders together, and sew in the sleeves (see "Finishing" on page 11). Pick up and k about 100 sts around the neck opening and rib for 1 inch in twisted ribbing (k1b, p1b) on size 2 dp needles with Dark Brown yarn. Bind off.

RED STARS PULLOVER

Rosemaling, a Scandinavian peasant style of decorative painting, rejoices in the so-called "farmer's" colors: tile blue, ocher, barn red, and moss green. These heavy, quiet colors are often used with bright colors like verdigris (the green of corroded copper), turquoise, scarlet, and light yellow. In this sweater, a bright scarlet glows beside the earthier tones of maroon, brown, and burgundy.

YARN: Worsted-weight wool at about 1000 yd/lb. The sweater shown is knit in Rauma Strikkegarn in the colors listed below.

CHART: page 98.

SIZES: To fit adult sizes S (M, L, XL, XXL). See page 87 for approximate measurements.

COLORS: 11 (13, 13, 15, 15) oz of Scarlet (color #124); 8 (9, 9, 11, 13) oz of Maroon (color #128); 4 (4, 4, 4, 4) oz of Burgundy (color #180); 8 (8, 8, 9, 9) oz of Red Brown (color #127).

GAUGE: 24 sts and 28 rnds = 4 × 4 inches.

SUGGESTED NEEDLE SIZE: Size 3 dp and 24-inch cir needles. Make a sample swatch on size 3 needles following one of the charts, and change needle size if necessary to get the proper gauge.

SLEEVES: Using dp needles, cast on 44 (48, 50, 52, 54) sts with Burgundy. Join and work twisted ribbing (k1b, p1b) for 2 (2, 2¼, 2¼, 2½) inches. In the next rnd, change to stockinette st (k every round) and inc 15 (17, 15, 19, 25) sts evenly to 59 (65, 65, 71, 79) sts. Always k the first and last sts in each rnd in the darkest color of that rnd to mark the underarm "seam". From here on, inc 1 st on each side of these "seam" sts every third (third, second, second, second) rnd until there are 137 (151, 163, 181, 187) sts. Work Chart 1 with Burgundy as the pattern color and Scarlet as the background. The chart shows where to begin the pattern after the "seam" sts. Then k 3 rnds in Burgundy. Work Chart 1 with Scarlet as the background, but change to Red Brown for the pattern color. Repeat Chart 1 with 3 rnds of Red Brown between the bands of pattern until the sleeve measures 20¾ (20½, 20¼, 20, 19¾) inches or desired length, including ribbing. Then p 1 rnd and k 7 rnds in Burgundy for the sleeve facing. Bind off. Make the other sleeve.

BODY: Cast on 254 (270, 290, 318, 342) sts with Maroon, join, and work a twisted rib (k1b, p1b) for 2¾ (2¾, 3, 3¼, 3½) inches. Change to stockinette st and k 3 rnds in Maroon. Always k

the first 2 and center 2 sts in each round in Scarlet to mark the side "seams". The charts show where to begin the pattern after the 2 "seam" sts. The background color will be Scarlet throughout, while the pattern color will vary. Work the first 24 rows of Chart 2 with Maroon pattern. Knit 3 rnds Scarlet, then work Chart 1 with Burgundy pattern followed by 5 rnds of plain Scarlet. Work Chart 1 with Red Brown pattern, then 3 rounds of Scarlet. Work Chart 2 in Maroon pattern until the body measures 21¼ (21¾, 22½, 23, 23½) inches or desired length to neckline. Bind off the center 33 (35, 35, 35, 37) sts, then continue working back and forth in stockinette st 1¼ (1½, 1½, 1½, 1½) inches. Bind off the same number sts at the center back. There will be 94 (100, 110, 124, 134) sts on each shoulder. Continue to knit both shoulders separately for 1 inch. Bind off.

FINISHING: Stay-stitch and cut the armholes, sew shoulders together, and sew in the sleeves (see "Finishing" on page 11). With dp needles, pick up and k about 92 (100, 100, 100, 104) sts in

Maroon around the neck opening. Join and k 1 round, p 1 rnd, then k for ¾ inch as a facing, increasing 1 st in each corner in every rnd so that the facing will lie flat against the inside of the sweater. Use a length of Maroon yarn with one ply removed (for less bulk) to sew the facing down inside.

STARS AND FLOWERS FOR A CHILD

Hand-dyed yarns have many nuances of color. It's hard to get exactly the same shade twice when hand dyeing. Today, we find such variation attractive, but do you suppose your great grandmother would have thought so? In this sweater, we've used two shades of every color to soften the dramatic contrast between hues.

YARN: Worsted-weight wool at about 1000 yd/lb. The sweater shown is knit in Rauma Strikkegarn in the colors listed below.

CHART: page 99.

SIZES: To fit sizes 3 years (6 years, 9 years, 12 years, adult S). See page 87 for approximate measurements.

COLORS: 2 (4, 4, 4, 6) oz of Mustard (color #150); 2 (4, 4, 4, 6) oz of Dark Blue (color #143); 9 (11, 13, 15, 15) oz of Honey (color #146); 8 (9, 11, 13, 13) oz of Midnight Blue (color #167).

GAUGE: 24 sts and 28 rnds = 4 × 4 inches.

SUGGESTED NEEDLE SIZE: Size 3 dp and 24-inch cir needles. Make a sample swatch on size 3 needles following one of the charts and change needle size if necessary to get the proper gauge.

BODY: Cast on 170 (182, 202, 226, 254) sts with Mustard. Join and k 1 inch for the hem. Always work the first 2 and center 2 sts of each rnd in the darkest color in each rnd to mark the side "seams". Then p 1 rnd and k 1 rnd. Mark the center front and center back with loops of contrasting yarn. Work Chart 1 once with Mustard background and Dark Blue pattern. The chart shows where to begin the pattern after the 2 "seam" sts. Then work Chart 2 with Honey background and Midnight Blue pattern, repeating until work measures 11¾ (13¾, 15¾, 18½, 22) inches or desired length, including hem. Bind off the center front 25 (31, 33, 33, 33) sts. Cast on 2 new sts over this area, forming a steek, so that you can continue to knit in the rnd; always p these 2 sts with both colors together. (When the body is finished, you will stay-stitch outside the p sts and cut open the neck between the machine stitching.) Work in pattern for 1¼ inches. Bind off the center back 25 (31, 33, 33, 33) sts. Cast on 2 sts over this bind-off to form a steek as you did in front and work 1¼ inches above the back bind-off. Bind off all sts.

SLEEVE: Using dp needles, cast on 35 (41, 43, 43, 43) sts with Mustard. Join and k 1 inch for a hem. P 1 rnd, then begin Chart 1 with Mustard as the background color and Dark Blue for the pattern. Always work the first and last st in each rnd in the background color to mark the underarm "seam". At the same time, inc 1 st on each side of these "seam" sts every third rnd.

Work the color pattern as follows: with Honey background and Midnight Blue pattern, work Chart 2 starting where an arrow indicates the size you have chosen. Continue until the sleeve measures 9½ (11¾, 14, 16¾, 19) inches or desired length above the p rnd, and there are 79 (95, 107, 121, 131) sts. Using Honey, purl 1 rnd, then k 1 inch plain for the sleeve facing. Bind off. Make another sleeve.

FINISHING: Stay-stitch and cut purled steeks at the front and armholes, sew the shoulders together, and sew in the sleeves (see "Finishing" on page 11). With dp needles, pick up and k about 80 (92, 96, 96, 96) sts around the neck opening in Mustard. Join and k 2 inches, increasing 1 st in every corner every rnd so that the facing will lie flat. The Mustard will be only slightly visible on the right side. Sew the facings down with Mustard yarn: split a length by pulling off one ply, creating a finer but strong yarn for sewing.

REDBIRD PULLOVER

In this sweater, geometric patterns are arranged with rows of archaically-stylized flowers and mystical birds. Such dissimilar patterns are often combined in folk art. The trellis and acanthus pattern are worked together here as an allover pattern.

YARN: Sport-weight wool at about 1600 yd/lb. The sweater shown is knit in Rauma Finullgarn in the colors listed below.

CHART: pages 100 and 101.

SIZES: To fit adult sizes S (M, L, XL). See page 87 for approximate measurements.

COLORS: 13 (15, 16, 18) oz of Burgundy (color #480); 13 (15, 16, 18) oz of Light Burgundy (color #499); 6 (6, 8, 8) oz of Turquoise (color #483); 2 (4, 4, 4) oz of Rust (color #434).

GAUGE: 28 sts and 32 rnds = 4 × 4 inches.

SUGGESTED NEEDLE SIZES: Size 1 and 2 each dp and 24-inch cir needles. Make a sample swatch on size 2 needles following one of the charts and change needle sizes if necessary to get the proper gauge.

BODY: Cast on 240 (252, 264, 282) sts onto size 1 24-inch cir needles with Rust yarn. Join and k 12 rnds for a hem, p 1 rnd, then work Chart 1 in Turquoise and Rust. Change to size 2 cir needles and inc 50 (62, 68, 78) sts evenly spaced to 290 (314, 332, 360) sts. Work the first 2 and middle 2 sts in every rnd in the darkest color in that rnd to mark the side "seams". Work Charts 2 and 3 with Burgundy background and Light Burgundy pattern. Continue Chart 3 until work is 16¼ (17, 17¾, 18½) inches from the p rnd. Then work Chart 4, knitting the first rnd with Burgundy background and Light Burgundy pattern. Continue with Turquoise background and Light Burgundy pattern. Then work Chart 5, the background in Turquoise and the birds and dots in Burgundy. Make four birds, one on each shoulder, front and back. Place the beginning of the first bird pattern (the outermost st of the wing) 4 (7, 12, 18) sts from the side "seam" sts. Fill in the area between birds with the double dot pattern shown in the chart. Begin the second bird 42 (45, 50, 56) sts from the other side "seam", maintaining the dot pattern as background. The outer edge of the second bird's wing will end 4 (7, 12, 18) sts from the other "seam" sts. Work the front and back pairs of birds with the same relationship of side "seams" and central field of dots. Knit birds and dots until the work measures 22 (22¼, 23, 23¾) inches from the p row. Bind off the center 48 sts in the front for the neck opening. To avoid knitting back and forth, cast on 5 new sts over the bound-off section. On every rnd, p these 5 sts with both strands of yarn together. When the body is finished, you will stay-stitch and cut along these 5 sts (see "Finishing", page 11). Continue the bird pattern for 1¼ (1½, 1½, 1½) inches more. Bind off the center 48 sts in back, and cast on 5 new sts to be purled with all colors used in each row. Finish the bird pattern chart and then work Chart 6 with Turquoise background and Rust pattern. Put all sts on a holder.

SLEEVES: Cast on 48 (48, 54, 54) sts with Rust on size 1 dp needles. Join and k 12 rnds for the hem, p 1 rnd, then begin Chart 1 in Turquoise and Rust. Change to size 2 dp needles and inc 13 (13, 5, 5) sts evenly spaced to 61 (61, 59, 59) sts. Work the first st of every rnd in the pattern color to mark the underarm "seam". Work Charts 2 and 3 with Light Burgundy as the background and Burgundy as the pattern color (the reverse of the pattern on the body), increasing 1 st on each side of the marking st every third (third, second, second) rnd until you have 167 (165, 189, 211) sts total. Work even until sleeve measures 20 (19½, 19, 19) inches or desired length from p rnd. Then work Chart 6 in Light Burgundy and Rust. Purl 6 rnds in rust for a facing and bind off. Make another sleeve.

FINISHING: Stay-stitch and cut the p sts at the neck, stay-stitch and cut the armholes, k the shoulders together, and sew in the sleeves (see "Finishing" on page 11). With Rust, pick up and k 7 sts for every 8 rnds along side of neck opening and each st bound off for the front and back neck. Join and work the bottom half of Chart 1 for the neck edge, decreasing 1 st in each corner of the neck opening in every rnd. In Rust, k 1 rnd, p 1 rnd, then k 5 rnds for the facing, increasing 1 st in each corner every rnd. Bind off. Sew in the sleeves. Sew down all facings, weave in all loose ends, and lightly steam press.

IRON GATE PULLOVER

This is an easy-to-knit sweater which shouldn't discourage even a beginning knitter. It has very little charted pattern in comparison to the others, but even so, the pattern has a lot to say. The inspiration for this design came from an old set of wrought iron door hinges.

YARN: Heavy worsted-weight wool at about 900 yd/lb. The sweater shown is knit in Rauma Vamsegarn in the colors listed below.

CHART: page 101.

SIZES: To fit sizes 9 years (12 years, adult S). See page 87 for approximate measurements.

COLORS: 11 (13, 15) oz of Yellow (color #V46); 4 (4, 4) oz of Dark Lilac (color #V81); 4 (6, 6) oz of Burgundy (color #V19); 4 (4, 4) oz of Turquoise (color #V83).

GAUGE: 20 sts and 24 rnds = 4 × 4 inches.

SUGGESTED NEEDLE SIZES: Sizes 5 and 6 each dp and 24-inch cir needles. Make a sample swatch on size 6 needles following one of the charts and change needle sizes if necessary to get the proper gauge.

BODY: Cast on 136 (152, 184) sts with size 5 cir needles and Yellow yarn. Join and k 11 rnds for a hem, p 1 rnd, then k 1 rnd. Work Chart 1 with Turquoise background and Burgundy pattern. On the next rnd, change to size 6 cir needles, Yellow yarn, and stockinette st; inc 44 (36, 36) sts evenly to 180 (188, 220) sts. Knit plain Yellow until the work measures 6 (7, 8) inches from the p row. From here on, work the first 2 and center 2 sts in each rnd in the pattern color to mark the side "seams". Work Chart 2 with Yellow background and Dark Lilac pattern. End by knitting Chart 1 with Turquoise background and Burgundy pattern. Keep the center 40 sts in front and back on the needles to knit a boat neck, and bind off the remaining 50 (54, 70) sts for each shoulder. Work each neck facing separately back and forth in stockinette st with Burgundy: k 3 rows, p 1 row, continue in stockinette for 6 more rows. Bind off.

SLEEVE: Cast on 28 (30, 30) sts with Burgundy on size 5 dp needles. Join and k 11 rnds for a hem, p 1 rnd, then k 1 rnd. Work Chart 1 with a Turquoise background and a Burgundy pattern. Change to size 6 dp needles and Yellow yarn. Place a marker on the first and last sts. Inc 1 st just after the first st and just before the last st of every other rnd until there are 86 (100, 110) sts. Continue until the sleeve measures 11¾ (13¾, 16¾) inches or desired length from the p rnd. Then work Chart 1 with Turquoise background and Burgundy pattern. Knit 1 rnd in Burgundy and bind off. (This yarn is too heavy to knit a facing at the top of the sleeve.)

FINISHING: Sew and cut the armholes, and sew shoulder seams (see "Finishing", page 11). Hem the bottom, sleeves, and neck facing. Work all loose ends into the back of the fabric and lightly steam press.

AUTUMN POINSETTIAS JACKET

The colors in this jacket lie near one another on the color wheel. To tickle the eye, the background and pattern colors are reversed on the sleeves and body. Color changes within the pattern needn't break up the whole; in this case, they make the pattern more intriguing.

YARN: Sport-weight wool at about 1600 yd/lb. The sweater shown is knit in Rauma Finullgarn in the colors listed below.

CHART: page 102.

SIZES: To fit adult sizes M (L, XL, XXL). See page 87 for approximate measurements.

COLORS: 15 (16, 18, 20) oz of Dark Lilac (color #470); 9 (11, 13, 15) oz of Dark Rust (color #428); 2 (2, 2, 2) oz of Light Rust (color #434); 2 (2, 2, 2) oz of Medium Rust (color #419); 4 (4, 4, 4) oz of Yellow Green (color #498).

GAUGE: 28 sts and 32 rnds = 4 × 4 inches.

SUGGESTED NEEDLE SIZES: Sizes 1 and 2, each in dp and 24-inch cir needles. For the beret, 16-inch cir needles in size 2. Make a sample swatch on size 2 needles following one of the charts and change needle sizes if necessary to get the proper gauge.

BODY: Cast on 251 (266, 286, 311) sts with Dark Lilac yarn on size 1 cir needles. Join, k 8 rnds for a hem, p 1 rnd, then k 1 rnd. Through the rest of the body, p the first 6 sts of each rnd using all strands together to form a steek to mark the center front, which you will later cut open.

Work Chart 1 with Dark Lilac background and Yellow Green pattern for the first 4 rnds, then 4 rnds with Dark Rust pattern and 4 rnds with Light Rust pattern. Change to size 2 24-inch cir needles and inc 59 (78, 92, 101) sts evenly around to 310 (344, 378, 412) sts. Work Chart 2 with Dark Rust background and Dark Lilac pattern. The chart shows where to begin the pattern for each size. Continue in pattern until the body measures 17¾ (18½, 19¼, 19¾) inches above the p rnd. Knit 1 rnd Dark Lilac, then work Chart 3 with Yellow Green background. The pattern is knitted in three colors: the diamonds and leaves are Dark Lilac while the rows of flowers are alternately Light Rust and Dark Rust. You will be knitting three colors in some rnds. Work the entire chart, then put all the sts on a holder.

SLEEVE: Cast on 45 (50, 50, 50) sts with Dark Lilac yarn on size 1 dp needles. Join, k 8 rnds plain, then p 1 rnd and k 1 rnd. Change to size 2 dp needles and inc 16 (9, 5, 25) sts evenly around to 61 (59, 55, 75) sts. Always knit the first and last sts of each rnd in the darkest color to mark the side "seams". Work Chart 2 with Dark Lilac background and Dark Rust pattern (the reverse of the body). Inc 1 st on each side of the "seam" every third (third, second, second) rnd until you have 127 (93, 201, 221) sts. For sizes XL and XXL, the sleeve is now fin-

ished. For sizes M and L, inc 2 sts as before every second rnd until you have 175 sts for size M and 191 sts for size L. For all sizes, work even until the sleeve measures 18½ inches or desired length from the beginning of Chart 2. Purl 6 rnds with Dark Lilac to make a facing. Bind off. Make another sleeve.

FINISHING: Machine stitch up the length of the body along the outside of the 6 p sts as described for sleeves in

"Finishing" on page 11, then cut between these lines of stitching to open the front. Starting at one edge of the p sts, count 59 (67, 75, 83) sts from the sts on the holder for the front shoulder; fold at that point to establish the arm edge and k the shoulders together. There will be 68 (70, 72, 74) sts remaining for the boat neck. Stay-stitch and cut the armholes (see "Finishing" on page 11). Turn the hem at the bottom of the jacket along the p row and sew in place.

FRONT/NECKBAND: Using size 2 24-inch cir needles, pick up sts along the entire front edge opening in Dark Lilac, picking up 7 sts for every 8 rnds (approximately 191 (196, 201, 206) sts along each front edge) plus the 74 (76, 78, 80) sts from back neck. Work the band using Chart 4. The direction of

the leaves reverses at center back, making the leaves mirror each other in front. You will only get whole leaves and a perfect mirroring of the pattern at center back if you have a multiple of 12 sts. To knit the band in the round, cast on 2 extra sts, forming a steek, at the bottom edge and purl them with all colors used in that rnd. When you're finished, machine st across them and cut them apart as you did for the front opening. Don't forget to change the leaf direction at these purl sts.

Work the wreath of leaves with Dark Lilac background; work the pattern in Dark Rust for 6 rnds, Medium Rust for 6 rnds and then Light Rust for 7 rnds. Work 4 rnds plain Dark Lilac, p 1 rnd, then end with 23 rnds plain in Dark Lilac for the facing. Machine stitch and cut open the p sts at the bottom. Sew the corners on the wrong side, turn them right side out, and sew down the facing. Sew in the sleeves. Sew all hems, weave in loose ends, and lightly steam press.

BERET: Cast on 144 sts on size 1 dp or 16-inch cir needles with Dark Lilac and join. For the band, k 12 rnds, p 1 rnd, then work Chart 4 in the same colors as the jacket band. Change to size 2 dp or 16-inch cir needles and Dark Lilac while you inc: *k 4, inc 1 between the fourth and fifth sts* (4 sts inc to 5). Repeat between *. Knit 6 rnds. Inc again: *k 5, inc 1 between the fifth and sixth sts* (5 sts inc to 6). Repeat between *. Knit 6 rnds. Purl 1 rnd, k 6 rnds. Begin decreases: k 5, k2tog around. Knit 6 rnds. Knit 4, k2tog around. Knit 6 rnds. Knit 3, k2tog around. Knit 6 rnds. Knit 2, k2tog around. Knit 6 rnds. Knit 1, k2tog around. Knit 2tog around. Break yarn, and with a yarn needle draw remaining sts up on the tail. Work ends into back of fabric.

RUST DAMASK JACKET

Subtle allover patterns are used with a broad band of strong contrasts to make both effects more striking.

YARN: Sport-weight wool at about 1600 yd/lb. The sweater shown is knit in Rauma Finullgarn in the colors listed below.

CHART: page 103.

SIZES: To fit adult sizes S (M, L). See page 87 for approximate measurements.

COLORS: 11 (13, 15) oz of Deep Rust (color #444); 9 (11, 13) oz of Medium Rust (color #419); 4 (4, 4) oz of Gray (color #4287); 2 (2, 2) oz of Light Rust (color #434).

GAUGE: 28 sts and 32 rnds = 4 × 4 inches.

SUGGESTED NEEDLE SIZES: Size 1 and 2 each dp and 24-inch cir needles. Make a sample swatch on size 2 needles following Chart 1 and change needle sizes if necessary to get the proper gauge.

BODY: Cast on 224 (264, 296) sts on size 1 cir needles with Medium Rust. Join and make a steek: in every rnd, p the first 4 sts using all the strands you are working with in that rnd. Later you will stay-stitch and cut along this line of p sts for the front opening. Rib k 1, p 1 for 2 inches. Change to stockinette st and size 2 cir needles and inc 20 (28, 32) sts evenly spaced to 244 (292, 328) sts. Work Chart 1 using Medium Rust background and Deep Rust pattern. Repeat the chart until the garment measures 24¾ (25½, 26¼) inches or desired length, including ribbing. Put all sts on a holder.

SLEEVE: Cast on 44 (44, 46) sts on size 1 dp needles with Medium Rust. Join and rib k 1, p 1 for 2 inches. Change to size 2 dp needles and inc 17 (17, 13) sts evenly spaced to 61 (61, 59) sts. Join. Knit the first and last sts in the darkest color in that rnd to mark the underarm "seam". Work Chart 1 with Medium Rust background and Deep Rust pattern. At the same time, inc 1 st on each side of the "seam" sts every third rnd until you have 159 (127, 93) sts. For sizes M and L, continue to inc 2 sts as before every other rnd until there are 175 sts for size M and 191 sts for size L. Work pattern on 159 (175, 191) sts until sleeve measures 18½ (18½, 19) inches or desired length from top of ribbing. Purl 6 rnds in Medium Rust for the facing and bind off. Make another sleeve.

ASSEMBLY: Machine stitch on each side of the center 4 p sts, then cut between the rows of machine stitching to open the front (see "Finishing" on page 11). Count 48 (60, 69) sts from the center front to locate each side "seam" and mark with basting thread. Machine stitch and cut the armholes at these lines as described on page 11. Knit the shoulders together, starting at the shoulders and working toward the neck. There will be a considerable gap at the center front and 52 sts remaining for the back neck.

NECKBAND: Using Gray, pick up sts for the neckband along the front edge and along the neck edge in back, picking up approximately 7 sts for each 8 rnds of knitting on the body, 166 (178, 178) sts each side, and 52 sts from the back neck. Try to end up with a multiple of 24 sts so the pattern will come out even. If you can't, place the pattern so that the center back is between two motifs. Add 2 extra p sts at the bottom so you can work the pattern in the round. Purl this steek in every rnd in both strands. Work Chart 2 with Gray background and Light Rust pattern for 22 rnds, then change pattern color to Medium Rust. End the neckband with 2 rnds of plain Medium Rust, p 1 rnd, then k 34 rnds in Medium Rust for the

facing. Bind off. Machine stitch and cut apart the 2 p sts as described on page 11. Sew bottom of band to bottom of facing along the inside of the sweater, then sew down the facing. Sew in the sleeves and sew down the sleeve facings and hems. Weave in all loose ends and lightly steam press.

FLOPPY CAP: Cast on 144 sts on size 1 dp needles with Medium Rust. Join and k 12 rnds, p 1 rnd, k 2 rnds. Work Chart 2 in the same colors as the neckband. Then continue in Medium Rust on size 2 dp needles, increasing as follows: k 4, inc 1 between the fourth and fifth st, around (4 sts inc to 5). Knit 6 rnds. Knit 5, inc 1 between the fifth and sixth st, around (5 sts inc to 6). Knit 6 rnds. Purl 1 rnd, then k 6 rnds. Dec for the floppy top: k 5, k2tog, around. Knit 6 rnds. Knit 4, k2tog, around. Knit 6 rnds. Knit 3, k2tog, around. Knit 6 rnds. Knit 2, k2tog, around. Knit 6 rnds. Knit 1, k2tog, around. Then k2tog around. Break the yarn with a 6 inch tail, then firmly draw up the remaining sts on this tail. Work all loose ends into the back of the fabric and hem the band. Lightly steam press.

IN THE NORWEGIAN WINTER

When winter settles over us with darkness, snow, and rain, we could use a little something to brighten up our lives! We have dedicated the sweaters in this chapter to good humor and vitality. We thought about summer, flowers, sunlight, birds, strawberries, and lace curtains blowing in a summer breeze.

CHILD'S REDBIRD PULLOVER

Strong, bright colors can easily become gaudy, but when all the colors used together are equal in strength, they keep one another in check. We've knitted two versions of this sweater, one with yellow and the other with light green background. We give both sets of colors, or you can choose other colors yourself.

YARN: Sport-weight wool at about 1600 yd/lb. The sweater shown is knit in Rauma Finullgarn in the colors listed below.

CHART: page 104.

SIZES: To fit child sizes 6 months (1 year, 2 years, 3 years, 6 years). See page 87 for approximate measurements.

COLORS: For Sweater A (with yellow background as in small photo, page 31), 4 (6, 8, 8, 9) oz of Yellow (color #431); 2, 2, 2, 2, 2) oz of Red (color #439); 4, 4, 4, 4, 4) oz of Dark Pink (color #465); 4 (4, 4, 4, 4) oz of Lavender (color #4088).

For Sweater B (with green background as in large photo, page 30), 4 (6, 8, 8, 9) oz of Green (color #455); 2 (2, 2, 2, 2) oz of Cyclamen (color #4886); 4 (4, 4, 4, 4) oz of Scarlet (color #424); 4 (4, 4, 4, 4) oz of Light Pink (color #479).

GAUGE: 28 sts and 32 rnds = 4 × 4 inches.

SUGGESTED NEEDLE SIZES: Sizes 1 and 2 each dp and 24-inch cir needles. Make a sample swatch on size 2 needles following Chart 1 and change needle sizes if necessary to get the proper gauge.

SLEEVE: Cast on 32 (34, 36, 40, 42) sts with A: Red or B: Cyclamen on size 1 dp needles. Join and rib k 1, p 1 for 1¼ (1¼, 1¼, 1½, 2) inches. Change to size 2 dp needles and stockinette st and increase 11 (9, 9, 7, 21) sts evenly to 43 (43, 45, 47, 63) sts. Work the first and last st of every rnd in background color to mark the "seam" and inc 2 sts every third rnd for all sizes, placing 1 inc on each side of the "seam" sts. Work Chart 1 with A: Yellow or B: Green background throughout, but alternate between A: Lavender and Dark Pink or B: Light Pink and Scarlet for each band of pattern for 4 (6, 7, 8, 10) bands. Knit 1 rnd A: Yellow or B: Green and continue in A: Red or B: Cyclamen until the sleeve measures 6¾ (8½, 10¼, 11, 13¾) inches or desired length, including the ribbing, and there are 71 (81, 93, 97, 125) sts. Purl 1 rnd, then k 8 rnds for a sleeve facing. Bind off. Make another sleeve.

BODY: Cast on 146 (162, 186, 198, 214) sts with A: Red or B: Cyclamen on size 1 cir needles. Join and rib k 1, p 1 for 1¼ (1¾, 1¾, 2, 2½) inches. On every rnd, work the first 2 and center 2 sts in the background color to mark the side "seams" and use yarn markers to indicate the center front and center back sts. Change to size 2 cir needles and stockinette st, and work Chart 1 in the same colors as on the sleeves for 3 (4, 5, 6, 7) bands of pattern. The chart shows where to begin the pattern after the "seam" sts for each size. Then work Chart 2 with A: Yellow or B: Green background and A: Red or B: Cyclamen pattern. Continue the rest of the body in Chart 1. When the body measures 8¼ (9½, 11, 11¾, 13¾) inches or desired length above the ribbing, bind off 11 (13, 15, 15, 15) sts at center front. Working back and forth in stockinette st, bind off at neck edges as follows: *size 6 months:* 3 sts at beginning of next 2 rows then 2 sts at beg of next 2 rows. *Sizes 1, 2, 3 years:* 3 sts at beginning of next 2 rows then 2 sts at beginning of next 4 rows. *Size 6 years:* 4 sts at beginning of next 4 rows then 3 sts at beginning of next 2 rows. To avoid a jagged edge when binding off several sts every row, slip the first st at the beginning of each row, k 1, then pass the slipped st over the k st. Continue to bind off as usual. Continue knitting 1¼ (1¼, 1¼, 1⅜, 1⅜) inches on remaining 125 (135, 157, 169, 177) sts. At center back, bind off 15 (17, 19, 19, 25) sts and continue each shoulder separately in stockinette st, binding off at each back neck edge only on every other row *size 6 months:* 2 sts once then 1 st once; *size 1, 2, 3, 6 years:* 3 sts once then 2 sts once. There will be 52 (54, 64, 70, 71) sts at each shoulder. Then work ½ (½, ½, ¾, 1¼) inch(es) on each shoulder, all the while continuing to work the pattern in Chart 1, but when there is no more room for whole patterns, work 1 rnd A: Yellow or B: Green and 1 rnd A: Red or B: Cyclamen until the body measures 10¼ (11½, 13, 13¾, 16¼) inches from the top of the ribbing. Bind off.

ASSEMBLY: Stay-stitch and cut armholes, sew shoulders together, and sew in the sleeves (see "Finishing" on page 11). Then pick up and k about 60 (68, 72, 76, 80) sts around the neck with A: Red or B: Cyclamen yarn and rib k 1 p 1 for 1 (1¼, 1¼, 1¼, 1¼) inches. Bind off. Work all loose ends into the back of the fabric.

DESIGN 9

FLOWER TRELLIS PULLOVER

Here three main colors are varied by using them in different ways. Green is used in three tones. Yellow and red have different emphases in each area of pattern; the band at the bottom of the body balances red and yellow equally, while the back is primarily red and the center front is mainly yellow. So these two colors give three completely different effects depending on how much of each color is visible. The cap, halfway between an ordinary ski cap and an alpine beret, is becoming to almost any head.

YARN: Sport-weight wool at about 1600 yd/lb. The sweater shown is knit in Rauma Finullgarn in the colors listed below.

CHART: pages 105 to 107.

SIZES: To fit sizes 9 years (12 years, adult S, M, L).

COLORS: 8 (9, 11, 13, 15) oz of Red (color #418); 8 (9, 11, 13, 15) oz of Yellow (color #412); 2 (2, 2, 2, 2) oz of Apple Green (color #454); 2 (2, 2, 2, 2) oz of Medium Green (color #458); 2 (2, 2, 2, 2) oz of Dark Green (color #432).

GAUGE: 28 sts and 32 rnds = 4 × 4 inches.

SUGGESTED NEEDLE SIZE: Size 2 dp and 24-inch circular needles. Make a sample swatch on size 2 needles following one of the charts and change needle size if necessary to get the proper gauge.

SLEEVE: Using dp needles, cast on 44 (48, 52, 56, 56) sts with Dark Green, join, k 1 inch for a hem, then p 1 rnd and k 3 rnds. With Medium Green and Red, work Chart 1 until the cuff measures 2¾ (2¾, 2¾, 3, 3½) inches from the p rnd. Change to Yellow and inc 29 (25, 21, 21, 21) sts evenly spaced to 73 (73, 73, 77, 77) sts. Work the first and last st of every rnd in the darkest color in that rnd to mark the underarm "seam". Inc 1 st on each side of these 2 "seam" sts every third rnd all the way up the sleeve. At the same time, work Chart 2 (the chart tells where to begin the pattern after the "seam" sts for each size) with Yellow background and Red pattern until the sleeve measures 9½ (11¾, 14, 13¾, 13½) inches or desired length above the cuff. Then k 3 rnds Dark Green, followed by Chart 3 with Apple Green as the background and Medium Green as the pattern color. Finish with 9 rnds of Chart 1 in Medium Green and Red followed by 7 rnds of Red. There should be 145 (157, 169, 171, 171) sts. Purl 1 rnd, then k 1 inch for a facing. Bind off. Make another sleeve.

BODY: Using cir needles, cast on 224 (252, 284, 300, 324) sts with Dark Green and k a 1 inch hem, then p 1 rnd and k 3 rnds. Work the first 2 and center 2 sts of every rnd in the darkest color in that rnd to mark the side "seams". Mark the center st front and back with a loose loop of a contrasting color. Work Chart 2 in Yellow background and Red pattern for 3½ (4, 4¼, 4¾, 4¾) inches. The chart shows where to begin the pattern after the "seam" sts for each size. Knit 1 rnd in Red while increasing 14 (14, 14, 14, 14) sts evenly spaced to 238 (266, 298, 314, 338) sts, then k 2 more rnds in Red.

Work Chart 3 with Apple Green background and Medium Green pattern as on the sleeve. Then k 3 rnds Red, and begin Chart 4 with Yellow background and Red pattern. The chart tells where to begin the pattern after the "seam" sts for each size. Work the central flower panel only on the front. Note that the center st of the flower panel should coincide with the center front st. When the body measures 15¾ (18¼, 22, 22¼, 23) inches or desired length to neckline, change to Apple Green and bind off 37 (37, 39, 41, 41) sts at the center front for the neck. Work back and forth in stockinette st for 3 rows with Apple Green, and then work Chart 3 with Dark Green background and Red pattern followed by 3 more rows of Apple Green. Work plain in Red until the shoulder measures 1¼ (1¼, 1⅜, 1½, 1½) inches above the front neck edge. Bind off 37 (37, 39, 41, 41) sts at center back. Work 1 inch more, working the 2 shoulders separately back and forth. Bind off remaining 82 (96, 110, 116, 128) sts on each shoulder.

ASSEMBLY AND FINISHING: Staystitch and cut the armholes, sew shoulders together, and sew in the sleeves (see "Finishing" on page 11). Then pick up and k approximately 106 (106, 108, 120, 120) sts around the neck opening with dp needles in Dark Green. Join and k 1 rnd, p 1 rnd, then k 8 rnds for a facing, increasing 1 st at each corner in every rnd so that the facing will lie flat on the wrong side. Sew down all facings and hems and work all tails into the back of the fabric.

CAP: These instructions are for a head measurement of 22 inches. For a child, dec the broad line of Red between pattern elements in Chart 5 from 3 to 2 sts, which will dec the circumference by ¾ inch. You must also cast on 6 fewer sts than for the adult size.

With dp needles, cast on 156 sts with Medium Green. Join and k 8 rnds for the hem, p 1 rnd, then k 3 rnds. Change to Yellow and k 1 rnd. Work Chart 5 with Yellow background and Red pattern. After you have worked the entire chart once, inc 2 sts (1 Yellow and 1 Red) on each side of each broad Red vertical stripe every third rnd, a total of 5 times, maintaining the striped pattern but not repeating the flowers. Inc by inserting the needle into the previous rnd of the first and last Red sts in the broad stripe, knitting with Red then Yellow, then knitting Red into the Red st on the left needle.

Now dec 2 sts on each side of the broad stripes every third rnd, a total of 7 times. Then dec 1 st at each wide stripe every second rnd until there are 8 sts left. Knit a 1¼ inch long cord in Red, then break the yarn. Using a yarn needle, draw the tail end of the yarn through the remaining sts and sew the tail into the inside of the hat fabric so that the cord forms a loop on the top of the hat. Hem the bottom.

BLOOMING CYCLAMEN PULLOVER

Here we borrow a design technique from lacemaking, where large patterns have to be held together and filled in with small patterns. This technique makes good sense in multicolor knitting, too. By overlaying a bold pattern on a finely patterned background, you avoid catching your fingers on loops of yarn inside the sweater. Notice how different each color looks when there is just a little of it than when there is a wide expanse of it.

YARN: Sport-weight wool at about 1600 yd/lb. The sweater shown is knit in Rauma Finullgarn in the colors listed below.

CHART: pages 107 and 108.

SIZES: To fit sizes 9 years (12 years, adult S, M, L). See page 87 for approximate measurements.

COLORS: 2 (2, 2, 2, 2) oz of Lavender (color #4088); 4 (4, 4, 6, 6) oz of Dark Violet (color #448); 8 (8, 9, 11, 11) oz of Midnight Blue (color #467); 8 (8, 9, 11, 11) oz of Light Blue (color #4385); 4 (4, 4, 4, 4) oz of Sea Green (color #4186); 2 (2, 2, 2, 2) oz of Hot Pink (color #4686); 2 (2, 2, 2, 2) oz of Cyclamen (color #4886).

GAUGE: 28 sts and 32 rnds = 4 × 4 inches.

SUGGESTED NEEDLE SIZES: Size 1 and 2 each dp and 24-inch cir needles. Make a sample swatch on size 2 needles following Chart 2 and change needle sizes if necessary to get the proper gauge.

BODY: Cast on 224 (252, 284, 304, 324) sts with Dark Violet on size 1 cir needles. Join and work 2/2 twisted rib (k2b, p2b) for 3½ (4, 4¼, 4¾, 4¾) inches. Change to size 2 cir needles. Knit 1 rnd and inc 14 (14, 14, 10, 14) sts evenly spaced to 238 (266, 298, 314, 338) sts. Always work the first 2 and center 2 sts in the darkest color of each rnd to mark the side "seams". With a loop of contrasting yarn, mark the center front st and center back st. Work Chart 1 with Sea Green background and Lavender pattern, followed by 3 rnds Hot Pink and 1 rnd of Midnight Blue. Work Chart 2 (the chart shows where to begin the pattern after the "seam" sts for each size) in Light Blue and Midnight Blue until the body measures 10¾ (13½, 16¾, 17½, 18) inches including the ribbing.

For the yoke, work Chart 1 with Sea Green background and Lavender pattern, then k 3 rnds Hot Pink. Work Chart 3 with Sea Green background and Dark Violet pattern for 20 rows (to the arrow at right of Chart 3), then change the pattern color to Cyclamen. At the end of Chart 3, k 3 rnds Hot Pink. Repeat Chart 1 with Sea Green background and Dark Violet pattern, then repeat it with Dark Violet background and Hot Pink pattern. When the body measures 15¾ (18½, 22, 22½, 23) inches or desired length from the base of the ribbing, begin the neck decreases as described below. End with 2 rnds of Dark Violet and bind off.

NECK DECREASE: Bind off 15 (15, 17, 17, 17) sts at the center front. "Neck Opening" on page 10 tells how to either knit back and forth here or to continue knitting around on a circular needle. Working in stockinette st, bind off at each side of the neck edge every other row or rnd as follows: *size 9, 12 years:* 4 sts twice, then 3 sts once. *Size S, M, L:* 4 sts once then 3 sts 3 times. Continue in stockinette st for 0 (0, ⅝, ¾, ¾) inch. Bind off 27 (27, 31, 31, 31) sts at center back. Working in stockinette st, bind off at each side of the back neck edge every other row as follows: *size 9, 12 years:* 3 sts once, then 2 sts once. *Size S, M, L:* 3 sts twice. Complete the color pattern, then bind off.

SLEEVE: Cast on 44 (48, 52, 56, 56) sts with Dark Violet yarn on size 1 dp needles. Join and work a 2/2 twisted rib (k2b, p2b) for 2¾ (2¾, 2¾, 3, 3½) inches. Change to size 2 dp needles and k 1 rnd while increasing 29 (25, 21, 21, 21) sts evenly spaced to 73 (73, 73, 77, 77) sts. Always k the first and last sts of each rnd in the darkest color of the rnd to mark the underarm "seam". At the same time, inc 1 st on each side of these "seam" sts every third rnd. Work Chart 1 with Sea Green background and Lavender pattern, then k 3 rnds in Hot Pink and 1 rnd with Midnight Blue. Work Chart 2 with a Light Blue background and a Midnight Blue pattern (the chart shows where to begin the pattern after the "seam" sts for each size) until the sleeve measures 12½ (15, 17½, 17, 16¼) inches above the ribbing. There should be 139 (153, 165, 167, 163) sts. Knit 5 rnds Lavender and 3 rnds Dark Violet, then p 1 rnd and k 1 inch for a facing. Bind off. Make another sleeve.

ASSEMBLY AND FINISHING: Assemble your sweater as described in "Finishing", page 11. Using smaller dp needles, pick up and k about 7 sts for every 8 rnds along the side neck edges and each of the bound-off sts along the front and back neck. Join and work a 2/2 twisted rib (k2b, p2b) for 1 (1, 1¼, 1¼, 1¼) inch. Bind off and work all loose ends into the back of the fabric.

FLOWERING RAGLAN PULLOVER

Notice the effect of changing the shade of green in different bands of pattern. Each green tone causes the others to stand out more clearly.

YARN: Sport-weight wool at about 1600 yd/lb. The sweater shown is knit in Rauma Finullgarn in the colors listed below.

CHART: page 109.

SIZES: To fit sizes 9 years (12 years, adult S, M, L). See page 87 for approximate measurements.

COLORS: 2 (2, 2, 2, 2) oz of Medium Green (color #458); 11 (13, 15, 15, 16) oz of Light Green (color #493); 2 (2, 2, 2, 2) oz of Cyclamen (color #4886); 2 (2, 2, 2, 2) oz of Hot Pink (color #4686); 2 (2, 2, 2, 2) oz of Red (color #424); 2 (2, 2, 2, 2) oz of Sea Green (color #4186); 13 (13, 15, 15, 16) oz of Dark Violet (color #448).

GAUGE: 28 sts and 32 rnds = 4 × 4 inches.

SUGGESTED NEEDLE SIZES: Size 1 and 2 each dp and 24-inch cir needles. Make a sample swatch on size 2 needles following Chart 1 and change needle sizes if necessary to get the proper gauge.

SLEEVE: Cast on 44 (48, 52, 56, 56) sts with Dark Violet on size 1 dp needles. Join and work twisted ribbing (k1b, p1) for 2¾ (2¾, 2¾, 3, 3½) inches. Change to size 2 dp needles and inc 29 (25, 21, 21, 21) sts evenly spaced to 73 (73, 73, 77, 77) sts. From this point on, always k the first and last st of each rnd in the darkest color of the rnd to mark the underarm "seam". Inc 1 st on each side of these "seam" sts every third rnd all the way up the sleeve. Knit 2 rnds with Dark Violet. Work Chart 1 with Medium Green background and Cyclamen pattern, then k 3 rnds with Dark Violet. Work Chart 2 with Light Green background and Red pattern, then k 3 rnds with Dark Violet. Repeat Chart 2, but with Sea Green background and Hot Pink pattern. End with 3 rnds of Dark Violet. Now work Chart 3 with Light Green background and Dark Violet pattern. Repeat this pattern until the sleeve measures 16¼ (18½, 21, 20½, 21) inches above the ribbing or desired length to armhole. There should be 159 (171, 185, 185, 189) sts. Bind off 14 sts centered at the underarm (the 2 "seam" sts plus 6 on either side). Put all remaining sts on a holder and set aside. Make another sleeve. Take care that the second sleeve ends at exactly the same point in the pattern as the first.

BODY: Cast on 224 (252, 284, 304, 324) sts with Dark Violet on size 1 cir needles. Join and work twisted rib (k1b, p1b) for 3½ (4, 4¼, 4¾, 4¾) inches. Change to size 2 cir needles and inc 14 (14, 14, 10, 14) sts evenly spaced to 238 (266, 298, 314, 338) sts. Knit 2 rnds of Dark Violet. Always work the first 2 and center 2 sts in each rnd with the darkest color in the rnd to mark the side "seams". With loops of a contrasting color, mark the center front and center back sts. Work Charts 1, 2, 2, and 3 in the same colors as the sleeves, with three rnds of Dark Violet at each change point. Work until the body measures 11½ (13½, 17, 17, 16¾) inches above the ribbing or desired length to armhole. Vary the length as needed to match the pattern exactly at the top of the sleeves. Then bind off 14 sts on each side, centered over the side "seam" sts.

RAGLAN YOKE: Place the sleeve sts on the needle on either side of the body where you have just bound off. At each point where the sleeve and body meet, k 2 sts in Dark Violet all the way up. Continuing the pattern, k around all the sts 3 more rnds. Then begin decreasing on each side of the lines of Dark Violet: k2tog in every rnd of the sleeve and every other rnd of the body until 136 (136, 140, 140, 140) sts remain, changing to size 2 dp needles when necessary. Change to size 1 dp needles and Dark Violet yarn, and work twisted rib (k1b, p1b) for 1 inch. Bind off, sew the underarm openings closed, and weave in all loose ends.

BIRDS ON A FENCE PULLOVER

To make a large pattern in more than one size without a lot of figuring, we placed the large pattern in the center of the front and back and surrounded it with a small vertical pattern that can be adjusted for size.

YARN: Worsted-weight wool at about 1000 yd/lb. The sweater shown is knit in Rauma Strikkegarn in the colors listed below.

CHART: pages 109 and 110.

SIZES: To fit adult sizes S (M, L). See page 87 for approximate measurements.

COLORS: 8 (9, 9) oz of Yellow Green (color #198); 6 (8, 8) oz of Cyclamen (color #173); 13 (15, 15) oz of Charcoal (color #1387); 2 (2, 2) oz of Orange (color #157).

GAUGE: 24 sts and 28 rnds = 4 × 4 inches.

SUGGESTED NEEDLE SIZES: Size 2 and 4 each dp and 24-inch cir needles. Make a sample swatch on size 4 needles following one of the charts and change needle sizes if necessary to get the proper gauge.

SLEEVE: Cast on 42 (42, 44) sts with size 2 dp needles and Charcoal yarn. Join and k 8 rnds for a facing, p 1 rnd, then k 1 rnd. With Charcoal background, work Charts 1, 2, and 3 using Orange, Cyclamen, and Orange, respectively, for pattern. Change to size 4 dp needles and inc 11 (7, 13) sts evenly to 53 (49, 57) sts. From now on, k the first and last sts of every rnd in Charcoal to mark the underarm "seam". Inc 1 st on each side of these "seam" sts every third rnd to 137 (91, 83) sts. Size S sleeve will then be finished. In the larger sizes, inc 2 sts as before every second rnd to 155 sts for size M and 167 sts for size L.

   Meanwhile, work Chart 4 with the background in Charcoal and the pattern in Cyclamen and Yellow Green. Then work Chart 1 with Charcoal background and Orange pattern. Then k the stripes of Chart 2 with 1 st Charcoal, 1 st Cyclamen until the sleeve is 17¾ inches long or desired length to upper border. Work Chart 1, then Chart 4 in the same colors as the wrist end of the sleeve. Purl 4 rnds and bind off. Make another sleeve.

BODY: Cast on 200 (216, 222) sts with Charcoal on size 2 cir needles. Join and k 8 rnds for the hem, p 1 rnd, then k 1 rnd. Work Charts 1, 2, and 3 as on the sleeve. Change to size 4 cir needles and Charcoal yarn, and inc 44 (52, 56) evenly spaced to 244 (268, 278) sts. The bird pattern in Chart 5 (Yellow Green background, Charcoal pattern) covers 93 sts in the center front and center back. Work the remaining sts in vertical stripes: k 1 Charcoal, k 1 Yellow Green. Repeat Chart 5 until the body is 4 birds high. Work Chart 4 with background in Charcoal and pattern in Cyclamen and Yellow Green, beginning at the arrow for your size. Edge this at both side "seams" with 2 sts in Charcoal all the way up. (This area will have three colors throughout. If this is too challenging, you may work the Yellow Green areas in Charcoal and duplicate st them in Yellow Green later.) Then work Chart 1 with Charcoal background and Orange pattern. Then k 1 Charcoal, k 1 Cyclamen stripes until the body measures 24 (24¾, 25½) inches from the p rnd.

BOAT NECK: Work the 60 sts in the center of the front back and forth in stockinette st with Charcoal to make the neck facing: k 3 rows, p 1 row, work 8 rows in stockinette st. Bind off. Repeat with the center back 60 sts.

ASSEMBLY AND FINISHING: Stay-stitch and cut the armholes (see "Finishing", page 11). Knit the shoulders together, hem the body and sleeves. Sew down the neck facing using yarn with one ply removed to reduce bulk. Sew in the sleeves. Work all loose ends into the back of the fabric and lightly steam press.

ALPINE MORTARBOARD: Cast on 125 sts in Charcoal with size 2 dp needles. Join. Work the band: k 12 rnds for the hem, p 1 rnd, k 1 rnd. Then work Charts 3, 4, and 1 (starting at the right edge of each chart) in the same colors as on the body. Knit stripes in Yellow Green and Charcoal while increasing at sts 1, 32, 63, and 94 (marking sts). Knit these marking sts in Charcoal throughout, and inc 1 st on each side of them in every rnd for 20 rnds. Then p 1 rnd even in Charcoal. Change to Cyclamen and Charcoal stripes and dec 1 st on each side of each marking st, every rnd until 10 sts remain. Break yarn and draw the remaining sts up on the tail. Work loose ends into the back of the fabric, hem the band, and lightly steam press.

CHARCOAL AND HOT PINK JACKET

Rows of leaves slip over into rows of flowers on this jacket. Letting one pattern take over from another so subtly creates a sophisticated look. The touch of charcoal on the edges enlivens the hot pink and orange pattern and sharpens the color changes.

YARN: Sport-weight wool at about 1600 yd/lb. The sweater shown is knit in Rauma Finullgarn in the colors listed below.

CHART: page 111.

SIZES: To fit adult sizes S (M, L). See page 87 for approximate measurements.

COLORS: 11 (13, 13) oz of Hot Pink (color #4686); 11 (13, 13) oz of Orange (color #469); 4 (6, 6) oz of Charcoal (color #4387).

GAUGE: 28 sts and 32 rnds = 4 × 4 inches.

SUGGESTED NEEDLE SIZES: Sizes 1 and 2 each dp and 24-inch cir needles. Make a sample swatch on size 2 needles following Chart 1 and change needle sizes if necessary to get the proper gauge.

SLEEVE: Cast on 45 sts with Charcoal yarn on size 1 dp needles. Join and k 10 rnds for the hem, p 1 rnd, and k 1 rnd. Work Chart 1 with Charcoal background and Hot Pink pattern for the first 7 rows, then Orange pattern for the rest. In the last row of Chart 1, change to size 2 dp needles and Charcoal, and inc 16 (16, 14) sts evenly spaced to 61 (61, 59) sts. For the rest of the sleeve, work the first and last sts of each rnd in Orange to mark the underarm "seam"; you will inc one st on each side of these "seam" sts every third rnd. Repeat Chart 2 with Hot Pink background and Orange pattern until there are 159 (127, 93) sts. Size S is now complete. Continuing the same color pattern on sizes M and L, inc 2 sts as before every *second* rnd to 175 sts for size M and 191 sts for size L. Work even until the sleeve measures 18½ (18½, 18¾) inches from the p rnd, or desired length to armhole. Bind off 14 sts centered on the "seam" sts. Put the remaining 145 (161, 177) sts on a holder. Make another sleeve.

BODY: Cast on 214 (228, 242) sts on size 1 cir needles with Charcoal yarn. Join and always p the first 2 and last 2 sts of each rnd with all yarns used in that rnd to make a steek through which to cut later for the front opening. Knit 10 rnds for the hem, p 1 rnd, and k 1 rnd. Work Chart 1 with Charcoal background and Hot Pink then Orange pattern as for the sleeves. Change to size 2 cir needles; with Charcoal yarn, inc 50 (62, 72) sts evenly spaced to 264 (290, 314) sts. Counting k sts out from the center purled area, mark the fifty-eighth (sixty-fourth, seventieth) st to each side of the center front to mark the side "seams". Always k these 2 "seam" sts in Orange. Work Chart 2 with Hot Pink background and Orange pattern. On the front, the pattern should be worked so that the first k st on either side of the p sts is the st marked "center front" on the chart. The chart shows where to begin the pattern for the back (after the "seam" sts). Continue until you have 12 leaves on each stem. For the underarm, bind off 14 sts on each side of the body, centering them on the line of Orange "seam" sts.

RAGLAN YOKE: On the cir needles holding the 236 (262, 286) body sts, position the 145 (161, 177) sts of each sleeve onto the bound-off armholes of the body, one sleeve per armhole, so that the right sides of the sleeves match the right sides of the body. Now continue the pattern following Chart 3, but with Orange background and Hot Pink pattern. Knit the 2 sts on the outside edges of each sleeve in Charcoal. (Use a separate little ball for each of these lines of sts, and anchor the yarn by "weaving it in" 1 st beyond the parting dec and as you come up on it, 1 st before the entering dec. This will make the Charcoal stitch lie nicely. If you have difficulty with this, you could use a loose marker for these points and k them in Hot Pink now, then work in a line of Charcoal duplicate st when you have completed the jacket.) On each side of these marking sts, dec by knitting 2 sts together in *every* rnd on the sleeves and *every other* rnd on the front and back. When only 140 sts remain, bind off.

FINISHING: Machine stitch on each side of the p sts of the center front steek and cut the front open as discussed for sleeves under "Finishing" on page 11. With Charcoal yarn and size 2 cir needles, pick up and k 140 sts around the neck opening. Cast on 3 extra sts at the center front and always p these. Afterward, you will machine stay-stitch along these stitches and cut them apart. Knit Chart 1 as on the body. Then k 1 rnd in Charcoal, p 1 rnd, and k 18 rnds in Charcoal for the hem. Bind off. Machine stitch on each side of the 3 p sts, cut down the center, and turn the band inside out to machine sew up the front edge to make a corner. Turn neckband right side out and hem the neckband.

With Charcoal yarn on size 2 cir needles, pick up and k 7 sts per each 8 rows of the body (including the neckband) along one front edge, inside the machine stitching. Cast on 2 extra sts at the bottom, then pick up the same number of sts along the other front edge and cast on 2 more sts at the top so that you can work the edges circularly. Always p the 4 extra sts with all strands in each rnd. Working sideways on the chart, match the front band pat-

tern to the neckband pattern and work Chart 4 in Charcoal background and alternating Hot Pink and Orange pattern. Then p 1 rnd, and k 15 rnds Charcoal for the facing. Bind off. Machine stitch through the p sts and cut the front bands apart. Sew the corners with the right sides facing, then turn and sew down the facing. Darn all loose ends into the back of the fabric and lightly steam press.

HAT: Cast on 140 sts on size 2 dp needles in Charcoal yarn. Join. Knit 12 rnds for the facing, p 1 rnd, k 1 rnd. Then work Chart 1 as you did for the body. Change to Hot Pink yarn. Mark sts 35, 70, 105, and 140 and dec 1 st on each side of them every other rnd until 4 sts are left. Change to Charcoal yarn and k around on these sts until you have a 1¼ inch cord. Break the yarn and draw the end through all 4 sts. Run the tail down inside the cord and darn it into the backside of the fabric. Hem the band and darn in all loose ends.

A LITTLE JUMPSUIT

Here three typical baby colors get a boost from a more definitive tone. The black makes the pastels less sweet without detracting from their cheerfulness.

YARN: Lace-weight wool at about 2600 yd/lb. The sweater shown is knit in Rauma Babyull in the colors listed below.

CHART: page 112.

SIZES: To fit child sizes 6 months (1 year, 2 years). See page 87 for approximate measurements.

COLORS: 8 (8, 8) oz of Light Pink (color #B79); 8 (8, 8) oz of Dark Pink (color #B45); 4 (4, 4) oz of Yellow (color #B20); 4 (4, 4) oz of Black (color #B36).

GAUGE: 32 sts and 36 rnds = 4 × 4 inches.

SUGGESTED NEEDLE SIZES: Size 00 and 1 each dp and 24-inch cir needles. Make a sample swatch on size 1 needles following Chart 1 and change needle sizes if necessary to get the proper gauge.

LEG: Cast on 48 (48, 50) sts in Black yarn on size 00 dp needles. Join and rib k 2, p 2 for 1½ inches. Change to size 1 dp needles and inc 31 (41, 49) sts evenly spaced to 79 (89, 99) sts. From this point on, k the first and last st of every rnd in the background color to mark the "seam". Inc 1 st on each side of these "seam" sts every third rnd. Work Chart 1 with Light Pink background and Black and Yellow pattern. Repeat the chart 2 (3, 4) times. Change to Chart 2 with Light Pink background and Black and Dark Pink pattern and repeat the pattern as you continue to inc. The pattern should be centered over the center st on the needle. When you have 123 (143, 163) sts and the leg is 9 (10¼, 11) inches long, bind off for the crotch: bind off the first 2 sts of the next row, k to the end, turn work around, bind off the first 2 sts and p to the end of the row. Repeat these 2 rows, maintaining the pattern while working back and forth in stockinette st, until 12 (14, 16) sts have been bound off on each side. Place remaining 99 (115, 131) sts on a holder. Make another leg.

BODY: Join the legs by putting the sts for both legs onto a circular needle. Purl 4 sts at the center front with both strands used in each rnd to make a steek which will be cut open later. Continue working Chart 2, and inc or dec 1 or 2 sts if needed to make the pattern match at the center back and center front. The pattern should be identical on both sides of the center front p sts. Continue Chart 2 until garment measures 15¼ (17, 19) inches. Bind off 14 sts centered over the center sts of each leg to make the armhole openings. Put the work aside and begin the sleeves.

SLEEVES: Cast on 28 (32, 32) sts in Black yarn on size 00 dp needles. Join and rib k 2, p 2 for 1½ inches. Change to size 1 dp needles and Dark Pink yarn. Inc 21 (19, 25) evenly spaced to 49 (51, 57) sts. Work the first and last st in every rnd in Dark Pink to mark the underarm "seam". Inc 1 st on each side of these "seam" sts every second rnd. Work Chart 2 with Dark Pink background and Light Pink and Black pattern until you have 95 (109, 129) sts. Continue without increasing until the sleeve is 5¼ (8½, 10½) inches long. Bind off 14 sts centered on the "seam" sts, and place the remaining sts on a holder. Make another sleeve.

RAGLAN YOKE: Add the sleeves to the cir needle in the bound-off openings of the body. There will be 332 (392, 464) sts. Mark the 4 "seams" where the parts meet by knitting 2 sts from the body and 1 st from the sleeve in Black on every rnd. On either side of

the Black "seams", dec 1 st every rnd from the sleeve and 1 st every second rnd from the body. (Make a little ball of Black yarn for each Black "seam" and use it when there is no Black in the rnd. Anchor the yarn from these balls 1 st before the entering dec and 1 st after the parting dec at each point.) Meanwhile, work Chart 3 in Dark Pink background and Black pattern, then Chart 4 in Dark Pink background and Yellow and Black pattern. Center the pattern of Chart 4 between each of the 4 "seams". When the garment is 19¾ (22, 24½) inches long, bind off 19 sts centered in the front for the neck. Work back and forth in stockinette st on remaining sts for 1¼ inches. Bind off 19 sts at the center back. Working each shoulder separately, continue the pattern while decreasing until no more sts remain on the sleeves (about ¾ inch). Put remaining (shoulder) sts on a holder.

HOOD: The hood is worked back and forth in stockinette st up to the crown, then is worked circularly. When finished, it is sewn onto the jumpsuit. On size 1 needles, cast on 18 sts in Black yarn on size 1 needles. Work 6 rows. From here on, work the 5 sts farthest to the left in Black, twisting the Yellow and Black yarns once to prevent holes. Work the rest following Chart 5 in Yellow with Dark Pink dots. When the piece is 1½ inches long, inc 1 Yellow st every row where the Yellow meets the Black until there are 32 sts. End with a p row. Lay this aside and make another piece exactly mirroring it, with the 5 Black sts on the outer right edge. Now join the two pieces: put both pieces together on one needle with the two Black edges together. Knit across the first piece, cast on 30 more Black sts between the pieces and k across the second piece (94 sts). Work 30 new sts and the 5 Black sts from each of the original pieces in Black for 6 rows; work the remaining sts in Yellow with Dark Pink dots. (The 30 Black sts are the lower back edge of the hood.) From here on, work the 30 Black sts in Yellow with Dark Pink dots. When the piece measures 3 inches at the side, dec for the face opening: dec 1 st each side where the Yellow meets the Black every second row 13 times (68 sts). Work

even for 2 (2¾, 3½) inches; then inc 1 st where the Yellow meets the Black every second row 6 times (80 sts). Cast on 13 new sts on one side, join the sides and continue Chart 5 working circularly on 93 sts. Knit 7 rnds and then begin to dec: k2tog, k 5, around. Knit 13 rnds. (Knit 13 rnds between dec rnds from here on.) Continue working the dots directly over the ones below, decreasing the distance between them as you dec. The next time you dec, k2tog, k 4; the next time, k2tog, k 3; the next time, k2tog k 2; then k2tog, k 1, the last time, k2tog around. Knit 7 rnds, break the yarn, draw up the remaining sts on the tail.

ASSEMBLY AND FINISHING: Staystitch and cut up the center front of the jumpsuit (see "Finishing", page 11). Sew the crotch seam. Knit the shoulders together. Sew the underarm seams. Backstitch the hood to the neckline. Pick up 8 sts for every 9 rows around the front opening and along the front edge of the hood with Black yarn. Rib k 2, p 2 for 2 rnds. To make buttonholes on the left, bind off 2 sts, k 6, bind off 2 sts, k 6, and so forth, up to just under the chin. In the next rnd, cast on 2 sts everywhere you bound off in the preceding rnd. Rib 1 more rnd and bind off. Make a Black tassel for the top of the hood. Darn all loose ends into the back of the fabric and lightly steam press. Sew on buttons opposite the buttonholes.

IN THE NORWEGIAN WOODS

We thought of trees, forests, wide horizons, cliffs by the sea, and Norwegian Gråstein apples as we designed these sweaters. To sheep's gray, sheep's black, and sheep's brown (the natural colors of wool) we added a number of blues and warm colors (like the skies and fruits of our natural world).

TONE'S SILVER BROOCH PULLOVER

Traditional silver brooches are worn all too infrequently in our country. They are wonderfully handsome and deserve to be worn more than the two days every year when all Norwegians dress up in traditional costume. The pattern on the front of this sweater is based on silver brooches. On the back and the sleeves are simpler allover patterns. This is an easy-to-knit sweater that would look great in almost any color combination.

YARN: Worsted-weight wool at about 1000 yd/lb. The sweater shown is knit in Rauma Strikkegarn in the colors listed below.

CHART: page 113.

SIZES: To fit adult sizes M (L, XL). See page 87 for approximate measurements.

COLORS: 15 (16, 18) oz of Gray Blue (color #168); 15 (16, 18) oz of Charcoal (color #107); 4 (4, 4) oz of Dark Blue (color #143).

GAUGE: 24 sts and 28 rnds = 4 × 4 inches.

SUGGESTED NEEDLE SIZE: Size 2 dp and 24-inch cir knitting needles. Make a sample swatch on size 2 needles following Chart 1 and change needle size if necessary to get the proper gauge.

BODY: Cast on 269 (289, 321) sts on cir needles with Dark Blue. Join and k 7 rnds for hem, p 1 rnd, and k 3 more rnds. From here on, always k the first 2 and center 2 sts in Charcoal to mark the side "seams", allowing 1 st more on the back than in the front to accomodate the patterns. Use Chart 2 for the front and Chart 1 for the back, both with Gray Blue background and Charcoal pattern. The charts show where in the pattern to start knitting for each size. When the body measures 24¾ (25½, 26¼) inches above the p rnd, or desired length to neck, bind off.

SLEEVE: With dp needles, cast on 47 (49, 51) sts with Dark Blue. Join and k 7 rnds for hem, then p 1 rnd and k 3 rnds. Work Chart 1 with Gray Blue background and Charcoal pattern. Knit the first and last sts of each rnd in Charcoal to mark the underarm "seam". Inc 1 st on each side of these "seam" sts every third rnd until the sleeve is 20 inches long or desired length. With Dark Blue yarn, k 3 rnds, p 1 rnd, then k 1 inch for facing. Bind off. Knit another sleeve.

ASSEMBLY AND FINISHING: Staystitch the armholes (see "Finishing" on page 11), cut them open, and sew in the sleeves. Sew the shoulders together, leaving about 11¾ inches open for the boat neck. With dp neeedles and Dark Blue, pick up and k about 140 sts around the neck and k 3 rnds, then p 1 rnd and k 6 rnds, increasing 2 sts at each side in every rnd so the facings will lie flat. Bind off. Hem neckline, wrists, and bottom edge, and work all loose ends into back of fabric.

NAVY ON PASTEL FOR A SMALL CHILD

This little pullover is easy to make—there are many colors but never more than two at a time. It's a wonderful pattern for using up little balls of leftover yarn. You can buy yarn for the pattern color and let your scraps become the background, although the scraps should have about the same weight and similar fiber content. You'll be surprised at the colors you can put together when you're knitting only narrow stripes of each.

YARN: Lace-weight wool at about 2600 yd/lb. The sweater shown is knit in Rauma Babyull in the colors listed below.

CHART: page 114.

SIZES: To fit child sizes 6 months (1 year, 2 years). See page 87 for approximate measurements.

COLORS: 4 (6, 8) oz of Navy Blue (color #B59); 2 (2, 2) oz of Medium Blue (color #B51); 2 (2, 2) oz of Light Blue (color #N72); 2 (2, 2) oz of Turquoise (color #B76); 2 (2, 2) oz of Lilac (color #B96).

GAUGE: 32 sts and 36 rnds = 4 × 4 inches.

SUGGESTED NEEDLE SIZE: Size 1 dp and 24-inch cir needles. Make a sample swatch on size 1 needles following Chart 1 and change needle size if necessary to get the proper gauge.

SLEEVE: With dp needles, cast on 36 (40, 44) sts with Navy Blue. Join and rib k 1, p 1 for 1¼ inches. Change to stockinette st and inc 15 (15, 15) sts evenly in the next rnd to 51 (55, 59) sts. Knit the first and last sts of each rnd in Navy Blue to mark the underarm "seam". Inc 1 st on each side of these "seam" sts every second rnd for the length of the sleeve. Work Chart 1 with Medium Blue background and Navy Blue pattern. The chart shows where to begin pattern for each size. Work Chart 2 using Navy Blue pattern throughout but shifting background as follows: 3 rnds Light Blue, 3 rnds Lilac, 3 rnds Light Blue, 3 rnds Turquoise, repeat. When there are 108 (129, 144) sts and the sleeve measures 6½ (8¼, 9½) inches or desired length including ribbing, p 1 rnd with Navy Blue, then k 8 rnds for the facing. Bind off. Make another sleeve.

BODY: Cast on 166 (186, 210) sts on cir needles with Navy Blue. Join and rib k1, p1 for 1¼ inches. Always work the first 2 and center 2 sts of each rnd in Navy Blue to mark the side "seams". The chart shows where in the pattern to begin for each size. Change to stockinette st and work Chart 1 with Medium Blue background and Navy Blue pattern, then work Chart 2 with

Navy Blue pattern and the same sequence of background colors as used on the sleeves. Work in pattern until the body is 10¼ (11½, 13) inches or desired length, including ribbing. Bind off 40 sts on each side for the shoulders, centered above the "seam" sts. Working back and forth with Navy Blue yarn for the remaining 43 (53, 65) front neck sts, k 1 row, p 3 rows, then work 8 rows in stockinette st for the neck facing. Bind off. Repeat this neck treatment for the back neck sts.

ASSEMBLY AND FINISHING: Stay-stitch and cut the armholes (see Finishing, page 11). Sew the bound-off sts together for the shoulders, then sew in the sleeves. Hem the neck edge in front and back. Work all loose ends into the back of the fabric. Lightly steam press.

SKI SWEATERS FOR THE WHOLE FAMILY

This sweater is very traditional in both the geometric patterns and the colors, but it will be richer if you use a variety of small geometrics. It will also be striking in sheep's black and natural white, or in colors to harmonize with your own outdoor wardrobe.

YARN: Sport-weight wool at about 1600 yd/lb. The sweater shown is knit in Rauma Finullgarn in the colors listed below.

CHART: page 115.

SIZES: To fit sizes 6 years (9 years, 12 years, adult S, M, L, XL, XXL). See page 87 for approximate measurements.

COLORS: 8 (8, 9, 11, 11, 13, 13, 15) oz of Charcoal (color #414); 8 (9, 11, 13, 13, 15, 15, 16) oz of Light Gray (color #404); 2 (4, 4, 4, 4, 4, 4, 6) oz of Medium Blue (color #437).

GAUGE: 28 sts and 32 rnds = 4 × 4 inches.

SUGGESTED NEEDLE SIZES: Size 1 and 2 each dp needles and 24-inch cir needles. Make a sample swatch on size 2 needles following Chart 1 and change needle sizes if necessary to get the proper gauge.

BODY: With size 1 cir needles, cast on 170 (190, 220, 230, 250, 270, 280, 310) sts with Medium Blue yarn. Join and k 16 rnds for the hem, p 1 rnd, and k 2 rnds. Work Chart 1 with Light Gray background and Charcoal pattern. Change to size 2 cir needles and inc 58 (50, 44, 58, 62, 66, 80, 74) sts evenly to 228 (240, 264, 288, 312, 336, 360, 384) sts. Work Chart 2 in the same background and pattern colors until work measures 13¾ (15¾, 18¼, 22, 22¼, 23¼, 23¾, 24½) inches or desired length to neckline above the p rnd. For the neck opening, bind off the center front 34 (36, 36, 38, 40, 40, 40, 42) sts. Working back and forth in stockinette st, finish the pattern element you've started, then work Chart 1. Halfway up Chart 1, bind off the same number of sts at the center back as you did in the front. Working the shoulders separately, finish Chart 1 and put all sts on holders.

SLEEVE: With size 1 dp needles, cast on 30 (40, 40, 40, 40, 40, 50, 50) sts with Medium Blue yarn. Join and k 16 rnds for the hem, p 1 rnd and k 2 rnds. Work Chart 1 with Light Gray background and Charcoal pattern. Change to size 2 needles and inc 7 (11, 15, 21, 21, 19, 14, 25) sts evenly spaced to 37 (51, 55, 61, 61, 59, 64, 75) sts. Always

k the first and last sts of each rnd in the darkest color in the rnd to mark the underarm "seam". Inc 1 st on each side of these "seam" sts every second (third, third, third, third, second, second, second) rnd until you have 133 (103, 115, 159, 127, 191, 201, 221) sts. Work Chart 3 with Light Gray background and Charcoal pattern. Sleeves in sizes 6 years, S, L, XL, and XXL are finished. For the other sizes, inc 2 sts every *second* rnd until you have – (139, 157, –, 175, –, –, –) sts. Continue even until the sleeve measures 12 (14¼, 16¾, 18½, 18½, 18¾, 18, 18¼) inches or desired length. For all sizes, purl 8 rnds for facing and bind off. Make another sleeve.

ASSEMBLY AND FINISHING: Stay-stitch and cut the armholes (see "Finishing", page 11). Knit the shoulders together. Sew in the sleeves. Pick up approximately 104 (108, 108, 112, 116, 116, 116, 120) sts around the neck with size 1 dp needles and Medium Blue yarn. Join and k 1 rnd, p 1 rnd, then k 8 rnds for the facing, increasing 1 st in every corner every rnd, so that the facing will lie flat. Bind off. Hem all hems, darn all loose ends into the back of the fabric, and steam press lightly.

CAP: Cast on 120 sts for a child's cap or 140 sts for an adult's on size 2 dp needles with Medium Blue yarn. Join and k 12 rnds for a facing, p 1 rnd and k 2 rnds. Work Chart 1 in the same colors as on the body. Inc 0 for child or 4 sts for adult sizes. Work Chart 2 for 6¼ inches for a child or 7 inches for an adult, measuring from the p rnd. Break yarn, thread the tail through all the sts (using a yarn needle) and draw up firmly. Work all loose ends into the back of the fabric and hem the bottom. Make a little Medium Blue pom-pom for the top if you wish.

BANDED PULLOVER

This sweater is knitted up in a jiffy because the same pattern is repeated throughout. Color variations add interest. Notice how the blue changes in character when placed next to brown or violet. The colors in this sweater recall the red of mountain ash berries on bare branches against a crisp blue October sky.

YARN: Worsted-weight wool at about 1000 yd/lb. The sweater shown is knit in Rauma Strikkegarn in the colors listed below.

CHART: page 116.

SIZES: To fit sizes 3 years (6 years, 9 years, 12 years, adult S). See page 87 for approximate measurements.

COLORS: 2 (2, 2, 4, 4) oz of Red (color #144); 2 (2, 2, 4, 4) oz of Deep Violet (color #112); 6 (8, 8, 9, 11) oz of Medium Brown (color #164); 6 (8, 8, 9, 11) oz of Gray Blue (color #151).

GAUGE: 24 sts and 28 rnds = 4 × 4 inches.

SUGGESTED NEEDLE SIZES: Size 2 and 4 each dp and 24-inch cir needles. Make a sample swatch on size 4 needles following the chart and change needle sizes if necessary to get the proper gauge.

BODY: With size 2 cir needles, cast on 166 (182, 202, 226, 254) sts with Deep Violet yarn. Join and k 8 rnds, p 1 rnd, and k 3 rnds. Change to size 4 cir needles. Always knit the first 2 and center 2 sts of each rnd in the darkest color of that rnd to mark the side "seams". Place a marker at the center front and the center back st. Work the bands of pattern as follows (the chart shows where in the pattern you should begin for each size): 1 band of the pattern with Red background and Deep Violet pattern, 1 band with Gray Blue background and Deep Violet pattern, then 1 band of Medium Brown background with Gray Blue pattern. Repeat the band with Medium Brown background for a total of 4 (5, 7, 8, 10) times. Work 1 band with a Gray Blue background and Deep Violet pattern, then a band with Deep Violet background and Red pattern. When you have worked the last Red rnd, bind off 31 (31, 33, 33, 33) sts centered in front for the neck opening and continue working either back and forth in stockinette st or circularly as described on page 11 for 1 inch. Bind off 31 (31, 33, 33, 33) sts at the center back and continue each shoulder for ¾ inch either separately back and forth or circularly by making another steek as described under "Neck

Opening" on page 10. Put the shoulder sts on holders.

SLEEVES: Cast on 35 (37, 39, 41, 43) sts with size 2 dp needles and Deep Violet yarn. Join and k 9 rnds for a hem, p 1 rnd, and k 3 rnds. Change to size 4 dp needles. Knit the first and last st of each rnd in the darkest color of that rnd to mark the underarm "seam". Work 1 band of the pattern with Red background and Deep Violet pattern. From now on, inc 1 st on each side of the "seam" sts every third rnd (in all sizes) for the length of the sleeve. Work the next band of pattern with Gray Blue background and Deep Violet pattern. Then repeat this band 4 (6, 7, 9, 10) times with Medium Brown background and Gray Blue pattern. End with one band in Deep Violet background and Red pattern. You should have 79 (95, 105, 121, 131) sts and the sleeve should measure 11 (14¼, 15¾, 19, 20½) inches from the p rnd. In Deep Violet, k 2 rnds, p 1 rnd, and then k 8 rnds for a facing. Bind off. Make another sleeve.

ASSEMBLY AND FINISHING: Stay-stitch and cut the armholes and k the shoulders together as described on page 11. Sew in the sleeves. Tack down all facings and hems. With size 2 dp needles and Deep Violet yarn, pick up and k about 84 (84, 88, 88, 88) sts around the neck edge. Join and k 1 rnd, p 1 rnd, then k 8 rnds for a facing, increasing 1 st in every corner every rnd so that it will lie flat. Bind off and hem the neck facing.

DESIGN 19

SANDAL-WOOD AND BLACK PULLOVER

We have used only two colors to show off the handsome pattern. The allover pattern and the band pattern are based on the same thematic shapes. Suggestions for creating such effects yourself are given in the chapter ''A Sweater is Born''.

YARN: Worsted-weight wool at about 1000 yd/lb. The sweater shown is knit in Rauma Strikkegarn in the colors listed below.

CHART: page 116.

SIZES: To fit adult sizes S (M, L, XL). See page 87 for approximate measurements.

COLORS: 16 (18, 20, 22) oz of Sandalwood (color #140); 16 (18, 20, 22) oz of Black (color #136).

GAUGE: 24 sts and 28 rnds = 4 × 4 inches.

SUGGESTED NEEDLE SIZES: Size 2 and 4 each dp and 24-inch cir needles. Make a sample swatch on size 4 needles following Chart 1 and change needle sizes if necessary to get the proper gauge.

BODY: Using size 2 cir needles, cast on 198 (216, 222, 246) sts with Sandalwood yarn. Join and k 8 rnds for a hem, p 1 rnd, then k 1 rnd. Work Chart 1 with Sandalwood background and Black pattern. In the last rnd of Chart 1, change to size 4 cir needles and inc 50 (52, 58, 62) evenly spaced to 248 (268, 280, 308) sts. Always work the first 2 and center 2 sts in every rnd in Black to mark the side "seams". Work Chart 2 once (the chart shows where in the pattern you should begin for each size), then repeat Chart 3 until the piece measures 23½ (24½, 25, 26¼) inches or desired length above the p rnd. Work Chart 4. To make a boat neck, keep 60 sts, exactly centered, in front and in back, on the needle and put the remaining sts on holders. Working each set of 60 sts separately back and forth with Black yarn, k 3 rows, p 1 row, then work 4 rows in stockinette st and bind off.

SLEEVE: Cast on 42 sts on size 2 dp needles with Sandalwood. Join and k 8 rnds, p 1 rnd, then k 1 rnd. Work Chart 1 with Sandalwood background and Black pattern. Change to size 4 dp needles and inc 11 (7, 13, 11) sts evenly spaced to 53 (49, 55, 53) sts. Knit the first and last sts of every rnd in Black to mark the underarm "seam". Work Chart 2 and then Chart 3 in the same colors while you inc 1 st on each side of the "seam" sts every third (third, third, second) rnd until there are 137 (91, 83, 179) sts. For M and L, continue to inc 1 st on each side of the "seam" every *second* rnd until you have 155 sts for size M and 167 sts for size L. The sleeve will measure 18 inches above Chart 1 for all sizes. Work Chart 4 for all sizes, p 6 rnds in Black for facing, and bind off. Make another sleeve.

ASSEMBLY AND FINISHING: Stay-stitch and cut open the armholes, knit the shoulders together from the inside, and sew in the sleeves as described on page 11. Work all loose ends into the back of the fabric and sew down all hems and facings. Lightly steam press.

CAP: Cast on 132 sts on size 2 dp needles with Black yarn. Join and k 12 rnds for the hem, then p 1 rnd and k 1 rnd. Work Chart 1 in the same colors as the sweater, then k only in Black for 2¾ inches. Dec: k2tog, k 6 sts, around. Knit 5 rnds even. Then k2tog, k 5 sts, around. Knit 5 rnds even. Knit 2 together, k 4 sts, around. Knit 10 rnds even. Then k2tog, k 3 sts, around. Knit 15 rnds even, then k2tog, k 2, around. Knit 15 rnds even, then k2tog around. Knit 15 rnds even, then k2tog around again. End by knitting 15 rnds, then break yarn, and with a needle draw the tail firmly through the remaining sts. Darn all loose ends into the back of the fabric and hem the bottom.

GEOMETRIC LIGHTS PULLOVER

Adding warm color to a single pattern element brings this otherwise rather somber pullover to life.

YARN: Worsted-weight wool at about 1000 yd/lb. The sweater shown is knit in Rauma Strikkegarn in the colors listed below.

CHART: page 117.

SIZES: To fit adult sizes S (M, L, XL, XXL). See page 87 for approximate measurements.

COLORS: 16 (18, 20, 22, 23) oz of Sheep's Brown (color #111); 15 (16, 18, 20, 22) oz of Purple (color #112); 2 (2, 2, 2, 2) oz of Black (color #136); 2 (2, 2, 2, 2) oz of Yellow (color #146); 2 (2, 2, 2, 2) oz of Cinnamon (color #181); 2 (2, 2, 2, 2) oz of Burgundy (color #128).

GAUGE: 24 sts and 28 rnds = 4 × 4 inches.

SUGGESTED NEEDLE SIZES: Size 2 and 4 each dp and 24-inch cir needles. Make a sample swatch on size 4 needles following the chart and change needle sizes if necessary to get the proper gauge.

SLEEVE: With size 2 dp needles, cast on 44 sts with Sheep's Brown yarn. Join and rib k 2, p 2 for 1 inch. Change to size 4 dp needles and stockinette st and inc 9 (5, 11, 9, 16) sts evenly to 53 (49, 55, 53, 60) sts.

Work Chart 1 with Sheep's Brown background and Purple pattern. (The chart shows where to start for each size.) As you work the sleeve, k the first and last st of each rnd with Purple to mark the underarm "seam" and inc

1 st on each side of these two "seam" sts every third (third, third, second, second) rnd. Work Chart 2, continuing with Sheep's Brown background and Purple pattern. The little diamonds (lights), represented by white circles in the diagram, are knitted first in Yellow, then in Cinnamon. Continue following Chart 2 until you have 137 (91, 83, 179, 190) sts. Sizes S, XL and XXL are now completed. For sizes M and L, continue to inc every *second* rnd until you have 155 sts for size M and 167 sts for size L. The sleeve will be 18 (18, 18, 18, 18½) inches above the ribbing. For all sizes, p 6 rnds in Sheep's Brown for a facing and bind off. Knit another sleeve.

BODY: With size 2 cir needles, cast on 200 (216, 222, 246, 268) sts with Sheep's Brown. Join and rib k 2 p 2, for 2 inches. Change to size 4 cir needles and inc 44 (60, 70, 62, 64) sts evenly to 244 (276, 292, 308, 332) sts. From here on, always k the first 2 and center 2 sts of every rnd in the darkest color of that rnd to mark the side "seams". Starting the pattern at the point indicated for your size, work Chart 1 with Sheep's Brown background and Purple pattern. Follow Chart 2 as for the sleeves, but repeating until you have worked diamonds in Yellow, Cinnamon, Burgundy, and Black. At this point, the body for all sizes will measure 24½ inches above the ribbing. For a shorter length, stop after the Burgundy diamond for a length of 20½ inches, or stop after the Cinnamon diamond for a length of 16½ inches. Change back to size 2 cir needles and Sheep's Brown yarn and rib k 2, p 2 for 8 rnds. Bind off 60 sts centered in both front and back for the neck opening, and put the remaining (shoulder) sts on holders.

ASSEMBLY AND FINISHING: Stay-stitch and cut the armholes as described on page 11. Knit the shoulder seams together and sew in the sleeves. Darn all loose ends into the back of the fabric and lightly steam press.

DOUBLE-BREASTED JACKET

Trees against the sky at dusk inspired this jacket—dark brown against several closely related sky colors.

YARN: Sport-weight wool at about 1600 yd/lb. The sweater shown is knit in Rauma Finullgarn in the colors listed below.

CHART: page 118.

SIZES: To fit adult sizes L (XL, XXL). See page 87 for approximate measurements.

COLORS: 11 (13, 15) oz of Brown (color #464); 6 (8, 9) oz of Lavender (color #4088); 4 (6, 8) oz of Gray Blue (color #451); 4 (6, 8) oz of Baby Blue (color #4385).

GAUGE: 28 sts and 32 rnds = 4 × 4 inches.

SUGGESTED NEEDLE SIZES: Size 1 and 2 each dp and 24-inch cir needles. Make a sample swatch on size 2 needles following Chart 1 and change needle sizes if necessary to get the proper gauge.

SLEEVE: Using size 1 dp needles, cast on 46 (48, 48) sts with Brown yarn. Knit 8 rnds for the hem and p 1 rnd. Work Chart 1 with Gray Blue background and Brown pattern, starting the pattern at the point indicated. Change to size 2 dp needles and inc 17 (7, 27) sts evenly to 63 (55, 75) sts. From now on, knit the first and last sts of every rnd with Brown to mark the underarm "seam", and inc 1 st on each side of these "seam" sts every third (second,

second) rnd. Work Chart 2, starting the pattern at the point indicated on the chart for your size. While the background is Brown throughout, the pattern color changes after each band of pattern: first Lavender, then Gray Blue, then Lavender, then Baby Blue; repeat. There are some rnds in the transition from one pattern band to the next where you will be using 2 pattern colors. Continue until there are 93 (201, 221) sts. Sizes XL and XXL are now long enough. For size L, continue increasing every *second* rnd, until there are 191 sts. The sleeve will measure approximately 18 inches from the beginning of Chart 2 for all sizes. With Brown, purl 1 rnd, k 8 rnds for a facing, and bind off. Knit another sleeve.

BODY: Using size 1 cir needles, cast on 362 (380, 392) sts with Brown yarn. Mark the center st with a loop of contrasting yarn; this is the center back. The first and last st in each rnd are always purled with both strands to make a steek that will be cut for the front opening later (see page 11). As the body is worked, double-breasted buttonholes are made to the right of the p sts: bind off 7 sts centered over the thir-

teenth st and again over the thirty-seventh st for the buttonholes, then in the following rnd, cast on 7 new sts above those you bound off for the buttonholes. Position the first row of buttonholes in the middle row of Chart 1 and then in the first (first, second) pattern band of Chart 2, followed by every other pattern band of Chart 2.

Join and k 8 rnds for the hem, then p 1 rnd. Work Chart 1 with Gray Blue background and Brown pattern. Change to size 2 cir needles and inc 24 (54, 90) sts evenly spaced to 386 (434, 482) sts. Work Chart 2 as on the sleeve. Work 7 (7, 8) bands of pattern. The body will measure 20 (20, 23) inches from the beginning of Chart 2. For the neck, bind off 98 sts in front centered on and including the 2 p sts. Cast on 2 new p sts over the bound-off sts and continue knitting circularly (see "Neck Opening" on page 11), or work back and forth in stockinette st for one-half of the next pattern band. Bind off 48 sts centered on the back marker and, working the 2 shoulders separately, work the rest of the pattern band. Put the remaining sts on holders.

ASSEMBLY AND FINISHING: Stay-stitch and cut between the purl sts in front (see "Finishing", page 11). Overlap the fronts to match the outer edges of the front and back neck openings to determine where the side "seams" should be, then stay-stitch and cut the armholes (see page 11). Knit the shoulders together. Sew in the sleeves. With size 2 cir needles, pick up and k sts along the front edges and around the entire neckline with Brown yarn: on the vertical edges, pick up 7 sts for every 8 rnds, and pick up all of the bound-off sts on the front and back neck edges. Add 2 purl sts between the bottom edges as a steek. Knit 1 rnd, then p 1 rnd. For the facing, k 8 rnds while decreasing 1 st every rnd at the top front corners and increasing 1 st every rnd in the corners of the neckline so that the facing will lie flat on the inside. Bind off. Stay-stitch and cut the purl sts of the steek at the bottom edge, then sew the facing down all around. Sew in the sleeves, darn all ends into the back of the fabric, and steam press lightly.

IN THE NORWEGIAN SPIRIT

This chapter, which is Lise's alone, is the only chapter in the book that doesn't build on the basic sweater shape. We wanted to show a few less familiar ways of making a sweater. Even when the approach is unfamiliar, knitters with a little experience should have no problems following our instructions. You can play with the designs in this chapter, or use them as rovings for spinning out your own ideas.

TAILORED JACKET WITH SADDLE SHOULDERS

The colors in this jacket remind us of logging roads edged with flowering goatweed. The jacket has a tapered bodice and dolman sleeves that slip into a saddle-shouldered yoke. The kimono collar is added after the rest of the jacket has been completed. Rolled down, it becomes a shawl collar with soft lapels.

YARN: Sport-weight wool at about 1600 yd/lb. The sweater shown is knit in Rauma Finullgarn in the colors listed below.

CHART: pages 119 and 120.

SIZES: To fit adult sizes S (M, L). See page 87 for approximate measurements.

COLORS: 11 (11, 13) oz of Cinnamon (color #425); 9 (9, 11) oz of Rose (color #465); 2 (2, 2) oz of Grape (color #442); 2 (2, 2) oz of Gold (color #431); 2 (2, 2) oz of Orange (color #461).

NOTE: This jacket would work well with shoulder pads.

GAUGE: 28 sts and 32 rnds = 4 × 4 inches.

SUGGESTED NEEDLE SIZE: Size 2 dp and 24-inch cir needles. Make a sample swatch on size 2 needles following Chart 1 and change needle size if necessary to get the proper gauge.

BODY: Cast on 234 (238, 242) sts with Cinnamon yarn on size 2 cir needles. Each side of the front uses 50 (51, 52) sts, and the back comprises 130 (132, 134) sts. The 4 remaining sts make a steek in the center front. Purl these 4 sts with all colors used in every rnd. Mark the 2 side "seams" by knitting 2 sts at each side in Cinnamon in every rnd. Join and, with Cinnamon, k 8 rnds, p 1 rnd, and k 1 rnd. Now k 1 rnd in Rose, then begin Chart 1 with Grape and Cinnamon as designated in the chart. Space the pattern so that you get a whole pattern element on each side of the purl sts in front and a division at the two side "seams". Continue with Chart 2, with Rose background and Cinnamon pattern, also spacing the pattern to get a whole pattern element on each side of the purl sts in front. At the same time, inc 1 st on each side of the "seam" sts (4 sts per rnd total) every second rnd until you have 260 (280, 302) sts. Continue knitting without increasing until the garment is 9 inches long. For the armholes, bind off 2 sts centered on the "seam" sts on each side. In the next rnd, cast on 2 new sts over those bound off. Purl these two groups of 2 sts from now on, using all colors in each rnd to form a steek, and continue to knit circularly. Now begin decreasing 1 st on each side of each of these 2 purl sts, (4 sts per rnd total) every second rnd until you have 152 (152, 174) sts. Knit even until the work measures 23 inches above the p rnd. Bind off.

SLEEVE: On size 2 dp needles, cast on 46 (48, 50) sts with Cinnamon yarn. Join and k 8 rnds for the hem, p 1 rnd, k 1 rnd. Work Chart 1 in Grape and Cinnamon as designated on the chart. Always k the first and last st of every rnd in Cinnamon to mark the underarm "seam" and inc 1 st on each side of these "seam" sts every 6th rnd until you have 66 (68, 70) sts, while knitting Charts 3 (with Rose background and Cinnamon pattern), 4 (with colors as designated on the chart), 5 (with Grape background and Cinnamon pattern), 4 (with colors as designated on the chart) 3 (with Rose background and Cinnamon pattern, and 1 (with Grape and Cinnamon as designated on the chart). Then begin Chart 2, with Cinnamon background and Rose pattern. Inc 1 st each side of the "seam" sts every rnd until you have 168 (170, 172) sts, then inc 1 st each side every second rnd until you have 180 (192, 194) sts. Knit even until the sleeve measures 21 inches above the p rnd.

TOP OF THE SLEEVE: Bind off 24 sts centered on the "seam" sts. In the next rnd, cast on 2 sts above the bound-off sts to form a steek. Always p these 2 sts with both strands of yarn in every rnd, and bind off sts as specified below on both sides of them while continuing to k circularly. This will leave a series of little holes along the steek, but later you will machine stitch outside the holes and cut the work open. * Bind off 6 sts at each side. Knit 3 rnds even.* For sizes M and L only, repeat from * to * once. For size S only, bind off 4 sts at each side and k 3 rnds even. Then for all sizes, bind off 8 sts on each side and k 3 rnds even. Then ** bind off 8 sts on each side and k 2 rnds even.** Repeat from ** to ** three times. Bind off 22 sts on each side. The 20 (20, 24) sts remaining on your needles are for the saddle shoulder.

SADDLE SHOULDER: Work the 20 (20, 24) sts in Chart 6 in Rose background and Cinnamon pattern, centering the pattern. When the saddle is 5½ (5½, 6¼) inches long, bind off 14 (14, 18) sts for the neck on the right side. Work the remaining 6 sts back and forth in stockinette st until the saddle is 7½ (7½, 8¼) inches long. Place the 6 sts on a holder. Knit the second sleeve, reversing the neck shaping by binding off for the neck on the left side of the saddle.

ASSEMBLY AND FINISHING: Lightly steam press. Machine stay-stitch and cut along the purl sts for the opening, armholes, and top of the sleeves (see page 11). Weave together the 12 saddle sts (6 from each saddle) where the shoulder pieces meet (saddle end to saddle end) at the back of the neck. Sew the long saddle edges to the body front and back, attach the sleeves, and darn in all loose ends. Hem the bottoms of the sleeves and the body.

KIMONO COLLAR: Using size 2 cir needles and Cinnamon yarn, pick up and k sts along the entire front and neck edge, picking up 7 sts for each 8 rnds along the front edges and approximately 1 st for each bound-off st around the neck. For the pattern to come out even, the number of sts you pick up should be divisible by 13. Cast on 3 extra sts at the bottom edge to make a steek. Join and work Charts 1, 3, 7, 8, 9, 4, and 10, using the colors specified on the charts and purling the 3 sts at the bottom edge with all colors used in each rnd. With Cinnamon, k 1 rnd, p 1 rnd, and then make the facing by working as many rnds in stockinette st as there are rnds before the purl rnd. Bind off. Machine stay-stitch and cut the kimono band at the steek. Turn the band inside out, fold it in half at the purl row, and stitch across each short edge to make a long, doubled facing. Sew the edges together at the bottom with right sides facing. Turn the facing right side out and sew it to the jacket, enveloping the cut front edge. Lightly steam press all seams.

CAP: (Not shown.) Cast on 130 sts in Cinnamon on size 2 dp needles. Join and k 20 rnds for the hem, p 1 rnd, then work Charts 1, 3, 7, 5, and 4. Purl 1 rnd in Cinnamon. Now dec on each side of sts 1, 37, 73, and 109 every rnd until only 12 sts remain. Break the yarn and draw it through the remaining sts. Pull up firmly and work the tail into the back of the fabric. Hem the bottom and work all tails into the back of the fabric. Lightly steam press.

BOLERO

This bolero is knitted circularly from wrist to wrist, but the central panel in the back is worked back and forth in stockinette. The colors are an explosion of golden harvest tones set against a cooler lilac and charcoal background: something to warm up in when the cold and melancholy settle over us late in the fall.

YARN: Sport-weight wool at about 1600 yd/lb. The sweater shown is knit in Rauma Finullgarn in the colors listed below.

CHART: pages 121 and 122.

SIZE: To fit adult size M. See page 87 for approximate measurements.

COLORS: 6 oz of Medium Violet (color #470); 2 oz of Light Rust (color #434); 4 oz of Medium Rust (color #419); 4 oz of Dark Rust (color #428); 4 oz of Charcoal (color #4387); 2 oz of Light Burgundy (color #499); 2 oz of Red Wine (color #497).

GAUGE: 28 sts and 32 rnds = 4 × 4 inches.

SUGGESTED NEEDLE SIZE: Size 2 dp and 24-inch cir needles. Make a sample swatch on size 2 needles following Chart 1 and change needle size if necessary to get the proper gauge.

BOLERO: Cast on 53 sts in Medium Violet on size 2 dp needles. Join and k 8 rnds for the hem, p 1 rnd, and k 1 rnd. For the rest of the sleeve, k the first st of each rnd in Medium Violet to mark the underarm "seam". Using Chart 1 with Medium Violet background, work three bands of leaves with Light Rust, then three with Medium Rust, and three more with Dark Rust pattern. At the same time, after knitting 1½ inches of Chart 1, inc 1 st on each side of the "seam" st every third rnd until there are 93 sts, then every rnd to 155 sts, then every second rnd to 209 sts, changing to cir needles when necessary. Continue on 209 sts until the sleeve measures 19½ inches from the p rnd. The "seam" st is now even with the hem of the jacket.

To begin the opening at the bottom of the body, cast on 1 st on each side of the "seam" st (211 sts total). Purl the "seam" and 2 new sts every rnd with both strands of yarn to form a steek that will be machine stitched and cut open later. Inc 1 st on each side of the purl sts every third rnd until you have 227 sts. Continue until you have worked Chart 1 nine times altogether. Following the pattern sideways from bottom to top, and continuing to work in a circle, begin Chart 2. First work the band of flowers with Charcoal background and Light Burgundy pattern. Then bind off 116 sts for the front opening, starting with and including the 3 purl sts.

The next band of flowers, with Charcoal background and Red Wine flowers, is the central panel of the back. Work it flat, back and forth in stockinette st on 111 sts. When that panel is complete (32 rnds), cast on 116 more sts for the left front of the bolero, including 3 purl sts for the bottom opening. (There will be 227 sts total.) Knitting circularly, work the final band of flowers in Chart 2 with Charcoal background and Light Burgundy pattern.

Begin the second sleeve with Chart 3 (the reverse of Chart 1, because you are now moving down the sleeve) in the reverse order of the colors you used on the first sleeve (Medium Violet background with pattern colors Dark Rust, then Medium Rust, and finally Light Rust). Meanwhile, dec the same number of sts you increased on the other sleeve: dec 1 st on each side of the purl sts every third rnd until you have 211

sts. Bind off the first and third purl sts in the steek, and from here on, k the center (remaining purl) st in Medium Violet to mark the side "seam". Dec 1 st each side of this "seam" every second rnd until you have 155 sts. Dec 1 st each side of the "seam" every rnd until you have 93 sts. Dec 1 st each side every third rnd until you have 53 sts. Work even 1½ inches, finishing Chart 3. Change to Medium Violet and k 1 rnd, p 1 rnd, and k 8 rnds for the hem. Bind off.

FINISHING: Stay-stitch and cut the purl sts open at the bottom of the bolero (as described for sleeves in "Finishing" on page 11). To make a facing for the entire edge, pick up and k approximately 500 sts in Charcoal yarn up one front, across the back neck, and down the other front edge, then across the bottom (about 7 sts per 8 rnds of knitting across the back neck and bottom edges and about 1 st for every st along the front edges). Knit 1 rnd, p 1 rnd. Then k 8 rnds while decreasing 1 st each rnd at the bottom front corners and increasing 1 st each rnd at each shoulder. At the same time, in every rnd inc 1 st on each side of the "seam" sts at each underarm to allow for the diagonal line of the bodice/sleeve. This will make the facing lie flat when you turn it in. Bind off, turn in, and sew down the facing. Hem the sleeves. Darn loose ends into the back of the fabric and lightly steam press the body.

With a yarn needle, embroider a chain stitch around the center of each flower, using Light Rust for flowers in Red Wine and Dark Rust for flowers in Light Burgundy.

HAT: Cast on 144 sts in Medium Violet on size 2 dp needles. Join and k 10 rnds for a hem, p 1 rnd, k 1 rnd. Work Chart 3 starting at the base of

the leaf, with 6, 6, and 7 rnds, respectively, of each pattern color (Light Rust, Medium Rust, and Dark Rust). Change to Medium Violet and k 1 rnd, p 1 rnd. Then begin to dec: k2tog, k 6 around; k 5 rnds plain; k2tog, k 5 around; k 5 rnds plain; k2tog, k 4 around; k 5 rnds plain; k2tog, k 3 around; k 5 rnds plain; k2tog, k 2 around; k 5 rnds plain; k2tog, k 1 around; k 5 rnds plain; k2tog around. Break the yarn, and with a yarn needle, pull the remaining sts up tight and fasten yarn into the back. Darn all loose ends into the back of the fabric and hem the bottom.

MAN'S JACKET WITH GEOMETRICS

We Norwegians associate pewter clasps with the somber sweaters worn to budget meetings of the king's cabinet at Staurgard. This jacket shows how effectively pewter clasps adorn a more modern man's jacket—one with a shaped body and set-in sleeves. On the body, the geometric pattern forms diamonds; on the sleeves, the same pattern moves in a zigzag.

YARN: Sport-weight wool at about 1600 yd/lb. The sweater shown is knit in Rauma Finullgarn in the colors listed below.

CHART: page 123.

SIZES: To fit adult sizes L (XL, XXL). See page 87 for approximate measurements.

COLORS: 13 (15, 16) oz of Antique Gold (color #417); 13 (15, 16) oz of Burgundy (color #480).

GAUGE: 28 sts and 32 rnds = 4 × 4 inches.

NOTE: This jacket is well-suited to shoulder pads.

SUGGESTED NEEDLE SIZES: Sizes 1 and 2 each dp and 24-inch cir needles. Make a sample swatch on size 2 needles following Chart 1 and change needle sizes if necessary to get the proper gauge.

BODY: Cast on 270 (300, 320) sts with size 1 cir needles and Antique Gold yarn. Join and rib k 1, p 1 for 8 rnds. Change to size 2 cir needles and stockinette st, and inc 36 (46, 56) sts evenly to 306 (346, 376) sts. Always work the first 2 and center 2 sts in Burgundy to mark the side "seams" and mark the center front by purling the 2 center front sts every rnd using both pattern and background yarns together to make a steek that will be machine stitched and cut open later. Work Chart 1 with Antique Gold background and Burgundy pattern, beginning the pattern after the "seam" sts at the position indicated for your size. Inc 1 st on each side of the "seam" sts (4 sts total) every tenth rnd until you have 346 (386, 416) sts. Continue until the sweater measures 12½ (13½, 14¼) inches above ribbing, or desired length to armhole. For the armholes, bind off the 2 "seam" sts on each side. In the next rnd, cast on 2 new sts above these and purl them in every rnd with both strands of yarn to make steeks and continue working circularly. Now dec 1 st on each side of these purl sts (4 sts total) every second rnd until you have decreased 21 sts on each side of the purl sts. You should now have 262 (302, 332) sts. Continue in pattern until piece measures 23 (24, 24½) inches above ribbing or desired length to neckline. Bind off 42 sts for the neck opening at center front, including the 2 p sts. Cast on 2 new sts over this gap to make another steek. Continue in pattern 1½ inches more, then bind off 40 sts in the center of the back. Cast on 2 sts above this gap to make a steek (purl these 2 sts with both strands in every rnd) and continue to work in pattern for 1¼ inches. Bind off.

SLEEVES: With size 1 dp needles cast on 48 sts with Antique Gold. Join and rib k 1, p 1 for 8 rnds. Change to size 2 dp needles and stockinette st, and work Chart 2 with Antique Gold background and Burgundy pattern. Always k the first and the last st in each rnd with Burgundy to mark the underarm "seam", and inc 1 st on each side of these "seam" sts every second rnd until you have 208 (212, 218) sts and the sleeve measures 20 (20½, 21¼) inches or desired length above ribbing. To begin the sleeve cap, bind off 14 (18, 22) sts centered on the 2 "seam" sts. Continue the pattern, knitting back and forth in stockinette st. At the beginning of the next 2 rows, bind off 14 (14, 16) sts. Then bind off 2 sts at the beginning of every row until there are 16 sts left. Bind off remaining sts.

ASSEMBLY AND FINISHING: Machine stay-stitch and cut along the purl sts in the front, armhole, and neck opening (see page 11). Sew the shoulders together. Sew in the sleeves. Knit a continuous facing for the neck and front with Antique Gold: pick up and k sts up one side of the front opening, around the back neck, and down the other side of the front opening. Pick up about 7 sts per 8 rnds of knitting along the fronts and about 1 st for each of the bound-off sts around the neck. Knit 2 rows. Work in stockinette st for 6 rnds, decreasing 1 st at the center front corners of the neck opening and increasing 1 st in each of the other corners of the neck opening in every rnd, so that the facing will lie flat. Bind off and hem the facing inside. Darn all loose ends into the fabric and lightly steam press. Sew on six pairs of pewter clasps evenly spaced along the front.

THE BIG, BIG TRIANGLE

This coat is certainly the most challenging of our sweaters to knit, but for sheer elegance it's worth the effort—and you'll probably never run into anyone wearing "your" coat! It's shaped like a big triangle; you start knitting at the bottom point, keep knitting circularly, and later cut openings for the hands and the center front. An alternative color combination might be two blues on a white ground, like fine china.

YARN: Sport-weight wool at about 1600 yd/lb. The sweater shown is knit in Rauma Finullgarn in the colors listed below.

CHART: page 124.

SIZE: To fit adult size M. See page 87 for approximate measurements.

COLORS: 22 oz of Dusky Rose (color #490); 15 oz of Antique Gold (color #417); 4 oz of Wooden Rose (color #440).

NOTE: This coat is well-suited to shoulder pads.

GAUGE: 28 sts and 32 rnds = 4 × 4 inches.

SUGGESTED NEEDLE SIZE: Size 2 dp and 60-inch cir needles. Make a sample swatch on size 2 needles following Chart 1 and change needle size if necessary to get the proper gauge.

TAIL: Start with dp 2 needles, with Dusky Rose background and Antique Gold pattern. Begin at the bottom point, in the center of the pattern element as shown on the small chart. Cast on only 1 st. Knit the small chart as shown back and forth in stockinette st.

An arrow at the bottom of the large chart shows where the pattern of the small, shaped chart fits into the continuation of the same pattern on the larger chart. As you begin the large chart, inc 1 st on each side every row until you have 83 sts, completing the tail of the cape.

From here on, work the 2 outermost sts on each side (the first and eighty-third) in Antique Gold all the way up the cape to mark the side "seams".

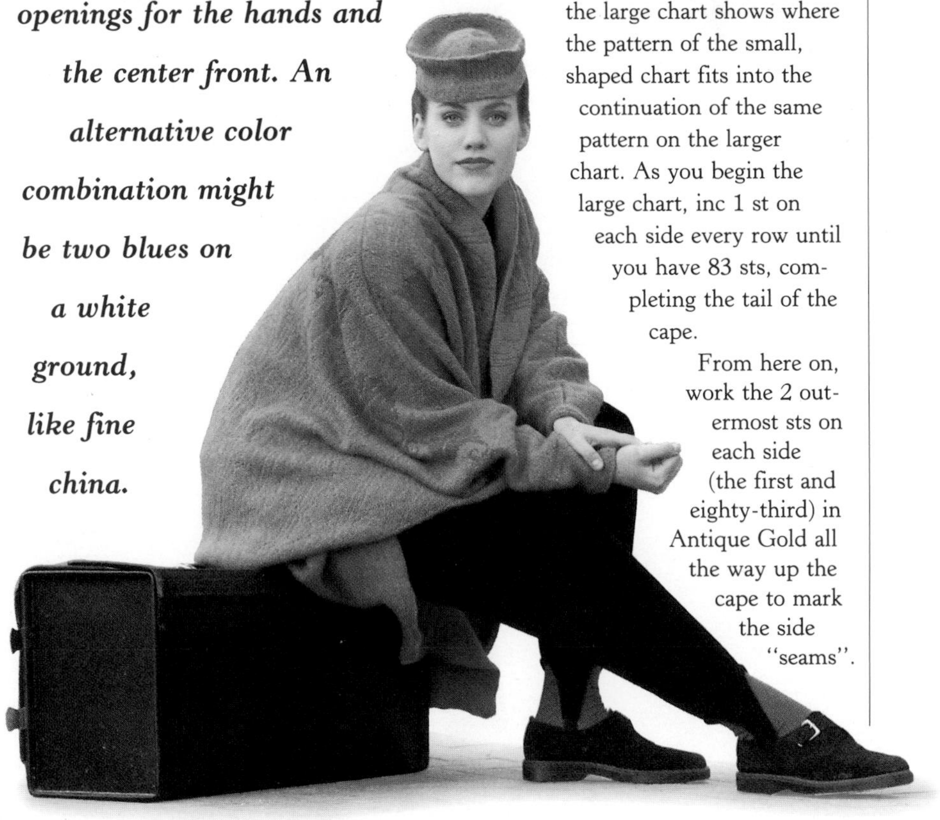

Make all side increases for both front and back on each side of these 2 lines of Gold sts. At the same time, begin to inc for the body.

BODY: Cast on a total of 6 sts for the beginning of the front at one edge of the 83 sts, join and begin knitting circularly on dp needles. Always p the 2 center sts of the 6 just cast on with both strands of yarn to make a steek along the center front, which you will later machine stay-stitch and cut open. Make all center front increases on each side of these purl sts. The sts cast on here with the center front increases and those on the forward sides of the Gold lines marking the side "seams" will become the front of the coat. The 81 sts between the gold "seam" lines with their increases continue in pattern for the back. Work the front of the coat in the established pattern. Make certain that the front pattern elements are mirror images on both sides of the central steek and between the Antique Gold lines (that is, the pattern is symmetrically placed between the Antique Gold "seam" sts starting from the point on the small chart and extending up the front).

Begin increasing at the side "seams"

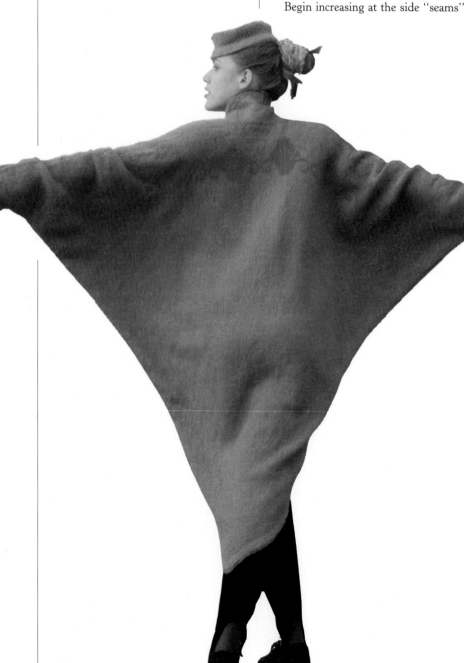

and center front at the same time. *On the sides,* inc 1 st every rnd for 2 rnds on each side of both Antique Gold lines (4 sts increased per inc rnd). Knit 1 rnd even. Repeat this sequence of increases (that is, 2 rnds out of every 3 are inc rnds.) *At center front,* inc 1 st on each side of the purl sts every third rnd. Transfer sts to cir needles when necessary.

When you have 307 sts, place a marker and stop increasing at the center front, but continue to inc along the side "seams" (4 sts total) every 2 of 3 rnds until you have 683 sts. Now inc 1 st every rnd on each side of the side "seams". After 3 rnds of these increases (695 sts), begin the base of the flower border as indicated on the chart. If you are not at exactly that point on the chart, you may begin the border a rnd or 2 earlier or later. Continue to inc 1 st every rnd on each side of the "seam" lines until the chart is completed and you have 767 sts. You are now at the wrists. For the wrists, add 38 sts to each sleeve for length: use both strands to cast on 38 sts centered over each of the 2 "seam" lines. On the next rnd, k 18 of these sts in pattern, then p 2 with both strands to make a steek, and knit the next 18 sts in pattern. (The purl sts will later be reinforced with machine stitching and cut apart to make the wrist opening.) When you reach the flowers themselves in the chart, knit them in Wooden Rose, with Antique Gold arches above the blossoms. Finish the chart and put all the sts on a holder. Congratulations! You did it!

FINISHING: Machine stay-stitch and cut the purl sts in front and at the ends of the sleeves (as described for armholes under "Finishing" on page 11). Knit the shoulders together, starting at the wrist and working toward the neck opening. The 36 sts remaining at the center back are for the neck opening.

KIMONO BAND: Beginning about 25 inches down from the top, at the marker where you stopped increasing for the center front, pick up and k about 380 sts in Antique Gold for the kimono band: up one side of the front, across the back of the neck, and down the other side. (Pick up about 7 sts for every 8 rnds on each side of the front opening and pick up each of the 36 back neck sts.) End opposite the point where you began.

To knit the band circularly, cast on 2 extra sts at the bottom. Purl these in every rnd with both strands together to make a steek which you'll machine stitch and cut apart later. Work the large chart, beginning where indicated by the arrow with Antique Gold background and Wooden Rose pattern, centering the pattern so that the sides match. Knit 36 rnds of pattern, then k 1 rnd in Antique Gold and p 1 rnd. Knit 36 rnds in Antique Gold to face the band. Bind off. Machine stay-stitch, cut, and sew the bottom edges, right sides facing. Hem the facing, enclosing the cut edge.

FACING: The tail also needs a facing at the lower edge. Pick up and k approximately 185 sts in Antique Gold beginning where the kimono band ends, then down around the point in the back and up to the band on the other side, again picking up about 7 sts for each 8 rows of knitting. Knit 1 rnd, then p 1 rnd. Knit 8 rnds, decreasing 2 sts every rnd at the center point of the tail so that the facing will lie flat when you turn it to the inside. Bind off, turn under the facing and hem it in place. To face the sleeve openings, use dp needles to pick up and k about 70 sts with Antique Gold yarn: k 1 rnd, p 1 rnd, and k 8 rnds for the facing. Bind off and hem the facings down inside. Work all loose ends into the back of the fabric and lightly steam press the coat. The weight of the yarn will cause the coat to stretch lengthwise when it is worn.

HAT: Cast on 140 sts on size 2 dp needles with Antique Gold yarn. Join and k 10 rnds for hem, p 1 rnd, then k 1 rnd. Work the portion of the chart indicated by the arrow with Antique Gold background and Wooden Rose pattern. The charted pattern doesn't come out even, so k the last st in each rnd in Antique Gold to mark the middle of the back with a "seam". Knit 24 rnds of pattern, a whole arch. Then k 1 rnd and p 1 rnd in Antique Gold. Change to Dusky Rose, then dec: k2tog, k 6 around. Knit 5 rnds even. Knit 2 tog, k 5, around. Continue to dec every 6th rnd, having 1 fewer st be-

tween k2togs until there are 0 sts between k2togs. Knit 2 tog around, break the yarn with a tail, draw the tail through the remaining sts and pull up firmly. Darn all tails into the back of the fabric, hem the bottom, and lightly steam press.

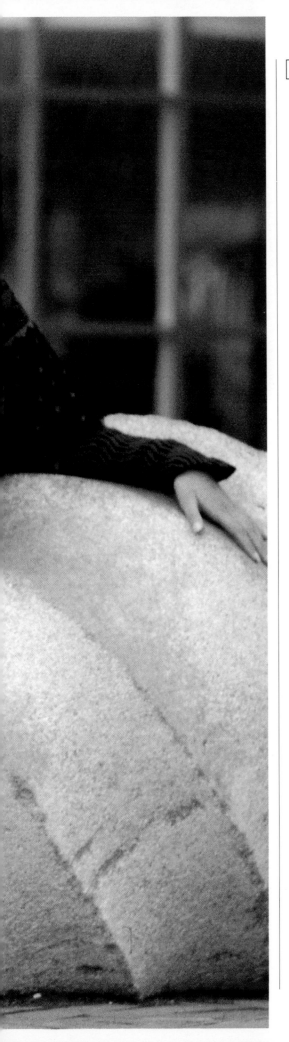

NORDIC CARVING SWEATER

Notice the scrolling vine and animal pattern slung over the shoulders surrounded by small geometrics. Does it remind you of ancient Viking woodcarvings or the great carved portals of Norwegian stave churches? This sweater is worked sideways, from hand to hand. It is first worked back and forth for a point on the back of the hand, takes off into circular knitting, and ends in a point on the back of the other hand. When you've finished knitting, you cut openings for the waist and the neck.

YARN: Sport-weight wool at about 1600 yd/lb. The sweater shown is knit in Rauma Finullgarn in the colors listed below.

CHART: page 125.

SIZES: To fit adult sizes S (M, L). See page 87 for approximate measurements.

COLORS: 9 (11, 11) oz of Blue (color #438); 4 (4, 4) oz of Light Rust (color #434); 9 (11, 11) oz of Black (color #436); 2 (2, 2) oz of Yellow Green (color #498); 2 (2, 2) oz of Cinnamon (color #425); 2 (2, 2) oz of Dark Rust (color #428).

GAUGE: 28 sts and 32 rnds = 4 × 4 inches.

SUGGESTED NEEDLE SIZE: Size 2 dp and 24-inch cir needles. Make a sample swatch on size 2 needles following Chart 1 and change needle size if necessary to get the proper gauge.

INSTRUCTIONS: Begin with Chart 1 with Blue background (blank squares) and Black pattern (circles), working the chart sideways. Cast on only 1 st, then inc 1 st on each side of this st every row until you have 57 sts. Arrange the sts on 3 or 4 dp needles and cast on 1 st, then k2tog to join them into a circle. Working circularly in stockinette st, k the first and last st of every rnd in Black. This pair of sts marks the underarm "seam": inc 1 st on each side of it every fourth rnd until you have 79 (81, 83) sts. Then inc 1 st on each side every rnd. Work Chart 2 in Black and Light Rust so that the Light Rust triangles point up the sleeve. Then work Chart 3 with Black background. The dots alternate colors: those in the first row are Cinnamon with Light Rust in the center; those in the next are Dark Rust with Yellow Green in the center. When there are 239 (241, 243) sts, continue to inc every rnd while working Chart 2 so that the Light Rust triangles point down the sleeve. There will be 243 (245, 247) sts and the sleeve will measure about 19¼ (19¾, 20¼) inches from the beginning.

You are now finished with the first sleeve. To knit the front and the back circularly, cast on 4 sts between the 2 "seam" sts and p these with both strands to make a steek which you will cut open later for the waistline. Work Chart 4 with Blue pattern and Black background starting at the point indicated for your size on the chart. At the same time, inc 1 st on each side of the purl sts every fifth rnd. After Chart 4, work Chart 2 again in Black and Light Rust, with the Light Rust triangles pointing toward the neckline. Then work Chart 1 in Blue and Black and continue to inc until you have 275 (279, 285) sts.

Now you're knitting the center front and back of the sweater. On the next row, k even to the nearest point in the pattern that makes a nice centerline; midway through one of the long verticals is good. Count the number of rnds you have knitted since the last inc and k just that many more rnds without increasing. Continue the same pattern, but *decrease* everywhere you increased before: dec 1 st each side of the p sts every fifth rnd while working Charts 1, 2, and 4 (reversing the direction of the figures) until you have 247 (249, 251) sts. Bind off the 4 p sts and draw the 2 Black "seam" sts close together in the next rnd. Dec 1 st on each side of this pair of sts every rnd while working Charts 2, 3, and 2 until have 79 (81, 83) sts. Change to dp needles when necessary. Then work Chart 1 and dec 2 sts every fourth rnd until you are down to 57 sts. Knit back and forth in stockinette st and follow Chart 1, decreasing 1 st on each side every row until no sts remain.

FINISHING: Sew and cut open the p sts at the bottom of the sweater (see page 11). With cir needles, pick up and k about 245 (262, 297) sts in Black along the bottom edge. Join and k 1 rnd, p 1 rnd, then k 8 rnds for the hem. Bind off, turn the hem under and stitch it down. With dp needles, pick up and k about 50 sts in Black around the end of each sleeve. Join and k 1 rnd, p 1 rnd. Then k 8 rnds while decreasing 2 sts every rnd at the point. Bind off, turn in, and hem. To make a boat neck 76 rnds long (9½ inches), first count out 38 rnds on each side of the center and mark the ends. Baste the cutting line with long sts and a contrasting yarn between the 2 center sts at the top of the shoulders. Machine staystitch just outside this center mark between the end marks, across 2 lines of knit sts at the ends, and back along the

outside of the center mark and across the other end. Make a second line of machine stitching just outside the first. (This stitching is lengthwise to your knitting, but crosswise on the garment.) Cut open the neckline between the machine stitching. With dp needles, pick up and k about 133 sts in Black along the entire neck edge (7 sts per 8 rnds of knitting). Join and k 1 rnd, p 1 rnd. Then k 8 rnds while increasing 2 sts at each end of the neckline in every rnd so that the facing will lie flat. Bind off and hem. Darn all loose ends into the back of the fabric and lightly steam press.

CAP: Cast on 126 sts on size 2 dp needles with Black yarn. Join and k 8 rnds for a hem, p 1 rnd, then work Chart 2, Chart 4, and Chart 2 again with the same colors as on the body. With Black yarn only begin decs: k2tog, k 5 around. Knit 5 rnds even. Knit 2 tog, k 4 around. Knit 5 rnds. Continue to dec every sixth rnd, having 1 less st between k2togs until there are 0 sts between k2togs. Then k2tog around. Break yarn with a 6-inch tail, and draw the remaining sts up on the tail. Darn all loose ends, including the tail, into the back of the fabric. Hem the bottom.

A DEAR LITTLE DRESS

A dear little dress with a flared skirt for an elegant young lady, knitted as a sweater with the skirt knitted on at the end. Notice the little red seeding that spreads farther and farther apart toward the bottom of the skirt.

YARN: Sport-weight wool at about 1600 yd/lb. The sweater shown is knit in Rauma Finullgarn in the colors listed below.

CHART: page 126.

SIZES: To fit child sizes 2 years (3 years, 4 years). See page 87 for approximate measurements.

COLORS: 6 (8, 8) oz of Lavender (color #4088); 4 (4, 4) oz of Yellow Green (color #498); 4 (4, 4) oz of Red Violet (color #496); 2 (2, 2) oz of Light Rust (color #434); 2 (2, 2) oz) of Deep Violet (color #474).

GAUGE: 28 sts and 32 rnds = 4 × 4 inches.

SUGGESTED NEEDLE SIZES: Size 1 and 2 each dp and 24-inch cir needles. Make a sample swatch on size 2 needles following Chart 1 and change needle sizes if necessary to get the proper gauge.

BODY: Cast on 184 (196, 212) sts on size 2 cir needles with Lavender. Join and work Chart 1 with Lavender background and Yellow Green pattern. Work the first 2 and center 2 sts in each rnd in Yellow Green to mark the side "seams". The chart shows where in the pattern to begin after the "seam" sts for each size. Work in pattern until the piece is 6 (6⅛, 6¼) inches long. Bind off the 2 "seam" sts on each side for the armholes. In the next rnd, cast on 2 new sts above the bound-off sts and purl these with both strands of yarn in all rnds to form two steeks that will later be machine stay-stitched and cut for the armholes. To shape the armholes, dec 1 st on each side of the p sts every rnd (4 sts per rnd) 10 (12, 15) times. Meanwhile, change to Chart 2 after the first (third, fifth) dec rnd. Continue to dec and work Chart 2 with the background in Red Violet and the pattern in Light Rust, Yellow Green, and Deep Violet as shown on the chart. When you have completed Chart 2, you will have 144 (148, 152) sts. Now work Chart 3. For the pattern to come out even, k 0 (1, 2) sts on the outside edges in both front and back (next to the p sts) in Lavender all the way up. The chart shows where in the pattern to start after the Lavender st(s). Chart 3 has Lavender background, while the pattern color changes with each row of flowers: first Red Violet with Yellow Green in the center, then Deep Violet with Light Rust in the center. Continue knitting until the work is 11½ (12½, 13½) inches long. Bind off 10 sts at the center front for the neckline. Working back and forth in stockinette st and maintaining the pattern, bind off 2 sts on each side of the neck every second row 3 times and then work even for ¾ inch. On the next row, bind off 20 sts at the center back, then work the 2 shoulders separately and bind off 2 sts at each back neck edge every second row, twice. Knit 2 more rows and put the remaining 94 (98, 102) sts for each shoulder on a holder.

SLEEVE: Cast on 28 (32, 36) sts on size 1 dp needles with Red Violet. Join and k 10 rnds for the hem, p 1 rnd and k 1 rnd. Work Chart 2 in the same colors as on the body. Change to size 2 dp needles and inc 22 (20, 18) sts evenly to 50 (52, 54) sts. Work Chart 1 in the same colors as on

the body, always knitting the first and the last st of every rnd in Yellow Green to mark the underarm "seam". Inc 1 st on each side of these 2 "seam" sts every second rnd until you have 118 (122, 130) sts. Work even in pattern until the sleeve measures 10 (10¼, 11) inches or desired length from p rnd. Now dec to fit the sleeve cap to the armhole: first bind off 2 sts at the underarm (the 2 Yellow Green "seam" sts). Working back and forth in stockinette st, dec 1 st at each end of needle every row. Change to Chart 2 after 1 (3, 5) dec rows. When Chart 2 is complete, 92 (92, 96) sts remain. Work 4 rows even in reverse stockinette st for a facing. Bind off. Make another sleeve.

SKIRT: Pick up 184 (196, 212) sts around the bottom edge of the body with size 2 cir needles and Lavender yarn. Knit 2 rnds. Inc 1 st, k 2 sts around. Knit 1 rnd of dots in rust: k 1 st Light Rust, k 2 sts Lavender. Knit 5 rnds plain Lavender. Inc on the sixth rnd: inc 1 st, k 3 sts around. Knit 1 rnd of dots with 3 sts between them, placing the dots directly above the previous ones. Knit 5 rnds even. Inc in the next rnd: inc 1 st, k 4 around. Then k 1 rnd of dots with 4 sts between the dots, with the dots again directly above those that came before. Knit 5 rnds. Inc in the next rnd: inc 1, k 5 sts around. Knit the next rnd of dots with 5 sts between dots. Knit 5 rnds. Then work Chart 2 with the same colors as before. Change to Red Violet yarn and k 1 rnd, p 1 rnd and k 11 rnds plain for a hem. Bind off and hem.

ASSEMBLY AND FINISHING: Machine stay-stitch and cut through the purl sts at the armholes (see page 11). Knit the shoulders together. With size 1 dp needles, pick up and k approximately 60 sts around the neck opening and work Chart 2. (The number of sts must be divisible by 4 for the pattern to come out even.) Then in Red Violet, k 1 rnd, p 1 rnd and k 11 rnds for a facing. Bind off and hem. Sew in the sleeves. Hem the sleeve facing over the cut edge, darn in the loose ends, and steam press lightly.

THE SWEATER CAPE

This sweater is knitted from hand to hand, while the cape is knitted like a skirt with the front panel knitted separately and sewn in afterward. We sewed the sweater and the cape together along the top of the sleeves, though that is not necessary.

YARN: Sport-weight wool at about 1600 yd/lb. The sweater shown is knit in Rauma Finullgarn in the colors listed below.

CHART: page 127.

SIZE: To fit adult size S (M,L). See page 87 for approximate measurements.

COLORS: For Sweater (Cape), 22 (6) oz of Black (color #436); 6 (22) oz of Light Burgundy (color #499); 2 (4) oz of Light Rust (color #434).

NOTE: This garment may be fitted with shoulder pads.

GAUGE: 28 sts and 32 rnds = 4 × 4 inches.

SUGGESTED NEEDLE SIZE: Size 2 dp and 24-inch cir needles. Make a sample swatch on size 2 needles following one of the charts and change needle size if necessary to get the proper gauge.

SWEATER: Begin with the sweater, which is worn under the cape. It's knitted crosswise, from wrist to wrist in the dot pattern. For all sizes, cast on 45 sts on size 2 dp needles with Light Rust yarn. Join and k 8 rnds for the hem, p 1 rnd, k 1 rnd. Change to Black yarn and work the dot pattern with Light Burgundy dots on a Black background, as shown on the chart. When the piece measures 1 (1½, 2) inches from the p rnd, begin to inc: place a marker between the first and last sts of the rnd and inc in the second st and next to last st in every third rnd until you have 83 sts, and then in every rnd until you have 155 sts. Change to cir needles when necessary. Inc 1 st each side every second rnd until you have 209 sts and the sleeve measures 18½ inches from the p rnd. The first sleeve is now finished.

Between the 2 marker sts, cast on 115 (119, 119) sts for the side of the body using method 2 as shown on page 9. Mark the center 3 of these new sts by purling them in every rnd to make a steek that will later be cut to open the bottom of the sweater. Continue in the dot pattern for 7½ (8¼, 9½) inches. Bind off for the neck: locate the shoulder (exactly opposite the purl sts), then bind off 11 sts on the front of the shoulder and 6 sts on the back. In the next rnd, cast on 3 new sts over the bound-off sts to make a steek. Purl these 3 sts in every rnd. Continuing in the dot pattern, dec 1 st each side of the p sts every third rnd. Repeat this 4 times. Knit 10 rnds even on remaining 300 (304, 304) sts. Now, *increase* 1 st each side of the p sts every third rnd. Repeat 4 times. Bind off the 3 p sts. Then cast on 17 sts: 11 on the front and 6 on the back. Knit even in pattern for 7½ (8¼, 9½) inches. The body is now complete and you are ready to begin the other sleeve.

Bind off 115 (119, 119) sts centered on and including the 3 p sts at the bottom of the sweater. You will have 209 sts. Now work the other sleeve in dot pattern making all decs at the underarm "seam", which will be very obvious at this point. However, place a marker there so you don't lose your place later. Dec 1 st on each side of the marker every second rnd until you have 155 sts. Dec 1 st on each side of the marker every rnd until you have 83 sts. Change to dp needles when necessary. Dec 1 st on each side of the marker every third rnd until you have 45 sts. Continue on 45 sts for 1¼ (1½, 2) inches and then change to Light Rust and k 1 rnd, p 1 rnd, and k 8 rnds for facing. Bind off.

FINISHING: Machine stay-stitch and cut between the p sts at the bottom and at the neck (as described on page 11). Sew the sides together. With Light Rust and size 2 cir needles, pick up and k about 285 (301, 301) sts (about 7 sts for every 8 rnds) along the bottom edge. Join and k 1 rnd, p 1 rnd, and k 8 rnds for a hem. Bind off. With size 2 dp needles, pick up and k about 80 sts around the neck in Black and k 11 rnds. Change to Light Rust yarn and k 1 rnd, p 1 rnd, and k 12 rnds for the facing. Bind off and sew the hems. Darn loose ends into the back of the fabric and lightly steam press.

CAPE: For all sizes, cast on 89 sts with Light Burgundy on size 2 dp needles. Always p the first and last st in every rnd with all strands of yarn used in that rnd to make a steek that will be cut open later. Join and k 2 rnds. Inc 1 st in every st (or between sts) to 178 sts. Knit 15 rnds even. From this point on, k 15 rnds even after every inc rnd. Work the inc rnds as follows:

k 2 sts, inc 1 st around to 267 sts;
k 3 sts, inc 1 st around to 356 sts;
k 4 sts, inc 1 st around to 445 sts;
k 5 sts, inc 1 st around to 534 sts;
k 6 sts, inc 1 st around to 623 sts;
k 7 sts, inc 1 st around to 712 sts;
k 8 sts, inc 1 st around to 801 sts;
k 9 sts, inc 1 st around to 890 sts;
k 10 sts, inc 1 st around to 979 sts;
k 11 sts, inc 1 st around to 1068 sts.

By the time the incs are completed, you should have worked 178 rnds. In the next rnd, inc after every 72 sts (14 incs) to 1082 sts. Work Chart 1 with Light Burgundy background and Black and Light Rust pattern. Change to Light Rust yarn and k 2 rnds, p 1 rnd, and k 8 rnds for the facing. Stay-stitch and cut the front open at the p sts (see page 11).

FRONT PANEL: With Light Rust yarn and size 2 dp needles, cast on 60 sts. Join and knit 8 rnds for the facing, p 1 rnd, and k 2 rnds. Then work Chart 2 with Light Burgundy background and Black and Light Rust pattern colors, centering the 47-st pattern on your knitting. (If you prefer to duplicate stitch the Light Rust in afterward, k the Light Rust sts in Light Burgundy now.) On the sts outside the charted pattern, k vertical stripes, alternating 1 Black st, 1 Light Burgundy st. Knit until the panel is as long as the front edge of the cape. Bind off. Machine stay-stitch along the third stripe from each side of the panel's charted pattern, cut the panel open, trim, and hand sew it into the front of the cape. Hem the entire lower edge.

NECKBAND: With size 2 dp needles, pick up and k 90 sts around the neck edge in Black. Join and k 8 rnds and

change to Light Rust. Knit 2 rnds, p 1 rnd, and k 10 rnds for the facing. Bind off and sew the facing on the inside. You may sew the cape to the sweater along the top of the sleeves and shoulders, starting at the neck on each side.

CAP: Cast on 142 sts with Light Rust on size 2 dp needles. Join and k 12 rnds, p 1 rnd and k 1 rnd. From here on, always work the first and last st in each rnd in Black to mark the center back. Work Chart 1 with Light Burgundy background and Black and Light Rust pattern. Then k 1 rnd in Light Burgundy. Change to Black and p 1 rnd. Change to Light Burgundy and begin the decreases: k2tog, k 6 sts around. Knit 5 rnds even. On the next rnd, k2tog, k 5 sts around. Continue to dec every sixth rnd, having 1 less st between decs, until no sts remain between the k2togs. Knit 2 tog around. Break the yarn, thread the tail through the remaining sts and pull up firmly. Darn all loose ends and this tail into the back of the fabric and hem the bottom.

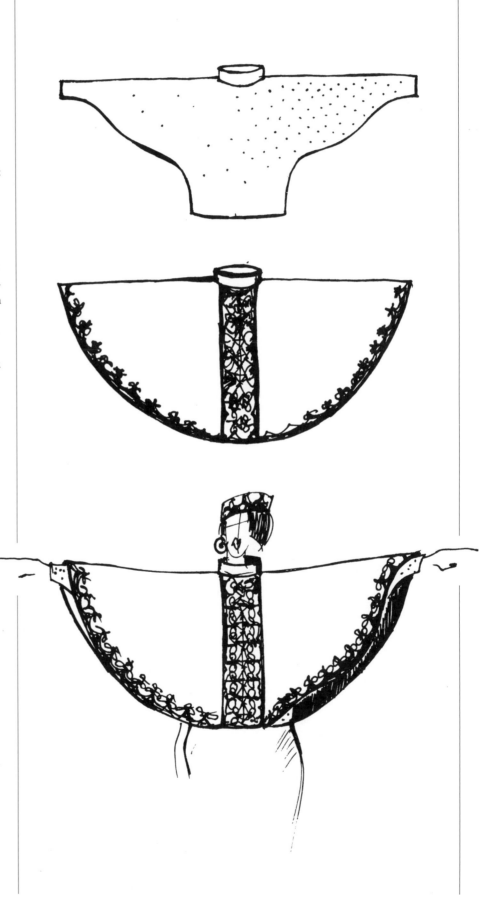

A SWEATER IS BORN

DESIGNING COLOR PATTERNS

The first step in creating your own Norwegian sweater is to design the charted patterns for it. You will need graph paper, ink, scissors, and glue. You can certainly use an ordinary school graph paper pad, but art and engineering supply stores have larger sheets with smaller squares, and graph paper proportioned for the difference in height and width of knitted stitches is also available. It is easier to get an impression of the pattern if the squares are roughly the same size and proportion as the stitches you will be knitting. A copy machine will help speed your work, but is not entirely necessary.

There are many ways to get started on a pattern. Here are some suggestions:

❖ Fill in squares to make a cross, a ring, a dash, or a square, and repeat the shape three or four times, evenly spaced. Add a new shape and draw it in, too, across your whole pattern. Keep filling in squares to make shapes until you are satisfied with your pattern.

❖ Make a grid of rectangular, diamond-shaped, bowed, or diagonal windows, photocopy it, and vary each copy by drawing different patterns in the windows. All these patterns will then have the same repeat, and can easily be used together on a single sweater.

❖ Use a detail from an embroidery or weaving pattern, a mosaic, or an antique knitted garment or knitting pattern. Improvise on it, put it into one of the window grids, or combine it with another pattern.

❖ Mark off a lot of little blocks, say 7× 7 or 13 × 13 squares. Fill each block with a different motif. Make 10 to 15 copies of the sheet, cut out all the little blocks and sort them. Try creating an allover repeat by placing many blocks together like a checkerboard, in stripes or bricks, or whatever repeat appeals to you.

❖ Paste up the patterns you like best onto a fresh sheet of paper. Make more copies and continue to improvise.

❖ Using a motif you especially like, see how many ways you can vary it. You can cut off some rows or columns of squares to make it shorter or narrower. You can cut the motif in half, mirror it, place it in a ring or a square, skew it into a diagonal. Or you can make positive and negative color changes, or turn alternate motifs upside down. The possibilities are almost endless. Using many repeats that are variations of one motif on a single garment has a special sophistication. You can use some as edge bands, side bands, or neckbands, and others as area patterns.

❖ With the help of two square pocket mirrors, you can discover many new patterns. Tape the mirrors together to form a right angle with the mirrors facing inside, and put them at various points on a motif. The mirrors then act as a kaleidoscope and create rosettes of pattern, which should give you a lot of great ideas. You can also just use one pocket mirror, placing it at different points on the motif to make a new bilaterally symmetrical motif.

TEST SWATCHES

When you have drawn up a number of repeat patterns that you like, it's time to find out how they will look knitted up. You must also decide what colors to use.

Use scraps of the same yarn you plan to use on the garment, or buy a ball or skein of each color you think you might want to use. On double-pointed or circular knitting needles, cast on 40 to 50 stitches (or more if your pattern is large). Join and knit around; it's quicker than flat knitting and gives a more realistic approximation of how many stitches you will have per inch if you plan to knit your sweater in the round. Your gauge can vary greatly, depending on whether you're knitting in the round or back and forth.

Try knitting your pattern in several color variations; your first color choice isn't always the best. As a rule, the more work you put into the planning and sampling, the more successful the finished garment will be.

If a pattern turns out to be difficult to knit or doesn't look as terrific as you thought it would, you have a number of choices. You can go back to the drawing board and work more on the pattern itself. You can embroider parts of the pattern in duplicate stitch instead of knitting them (see the chapter titled "Knitting Techniques"). Or you can toss out that entire pattern. But save the swatch you've knitted; you've learned something from it, and you may get new ideas later using that swatch as a starting point.

Besides color and pattern, a swatch will also show you how the fabric feels. It should be neither too open nor too firm. Try out various sizes of knitting needles on different swatches and label each swatch with the size needles you used.

In a notebook, record the yarn used, needle sizes, ideas about changes for the next time, and thoughts about the colors you used. If you do this with every swatch you knit, you'll avoid repeating mistakes. No one says you *have* to knit a mountain of swatches every time you plan to knit a garment. Do as much with it as you want, but we guarantee that the more work you put into drawing patterns and trying out colors, the more fun you will have knitting the results!

KNITTING GAUGE

When you have found a knitting gauge you like—when the firmness of the knitting and the quality of the fabric pleases you—it's time to start counting stitches. Steam press the swatches lightly and with straight pins, mark off 4 inches both widthwise and lengthwise. Cut open the tube of knitting if it is less than 4 inches wide. Count how many stitches and rounds there are in the two 4-inch directions. This is your personal knitting gauge. Note the needle size and yarn type you used.

BASIC DESIGN

Now it's time to make a basic paper pattern. It's easiest to start out with the table of measurements on page 87 or a sweater of your own that fits nicely. Using brown paper, draw around the garment or lay out a paper pattern based on the measurements given on page 87 for our basic patterns. Compare the drawing to your own measurements: measure the width around your hips and bustline, and measure the length from the back of your neck to the length that you want the sweater to be. If necessary, adjust the drawing to accommodate your measurements.

The basic shape we have used for our directions do not follow every curve of the body; they include extra width for ease. If you want more or less ease than we have allowed, correct for this on your paper pattern.

To determine the sleeve length, it's not enough to measure from the shoulder seam on the sweater body to the end of the wrist and compare it with the sleeve measurement from your shoulder tip to your wrist. Because the body of the garment has extra width designed into it, its shoulder will fall well below your shoulder. Instead, measure the length from the base of one hand, across your shoulders, to the other hand with your elbows slightly bent. Compare this figure with the same measurement from one sleeve end then across the body width to the other sleeve end on the paper pattern. If the body of your sweater is not as wide as our measurements, you will need to make your sleeves longer; if the body of your sweater is wider than ours, make your sleeves shorter.

When you have adjusted the paper pattern to your satisfaction, draw in the final lines with a thick pencil, crayon, or marker. Now paste sheets of tissue or butcher paper together to make a couple of sheets large enough to cover your basic pattern. Trace the pattern onto each of these sheets and sketch on them how the final sweater will look.

Think through where the bands of pattern should be placed, which colors to use, how the neck, sleeve, and waist edges will be finished, and so forth, and note this information on your sketch.

The first few times you make your own sweaters from scratch, it might be useful to photocopy the actual color patterns and paste them directly onto the sketch.

YOUR PERSONAL BASIC INSTRUCTIONS

You can make your personal set of knitting instructions to use for many sweaters simply by combining your body measurements (or the standard body measurements on page 87) with your personal knitting gauge. For a sweater to fit as you planned, your gauge swatch must be *in the yarn and color pattern you plan to use*. In the next section, you will learn to adapt these instructions to particular sweaters.

To find out how many stitches you will need for the body, multiply the number of stitches per inch in your swatch by the circumference you want. Multiplying the number of rounds per inch in your swatch by the length you want will give you the number of rounds you will need.

For example, let's say that you want to knit a sweater from Rauma Finullgarn, beginning with the sleeve. From your test swatch you know that you knit 28 stitches and 32 rounds in a 4-inch square. Dividing the number of sts by 4 inches gives you the number of sts you knit per inch: 28 divided by 4 = 7; thus, you knit 7 sts per inch with this yarn. To find how many sts to cast on at the bottom of your sleeve, you can either measure your own wrist or use the standard wrist measurement for your size from the table on page 87. For example, size Medium has a wrist measurement of 7¾ inches. Multiply: 7¾ (inches) × 7 (stitches per inch) = 54¼ stitches. At this point (and not before), you should round off to the nearest whole number. You will cast on 54 sts for the sleeve.

To fit a pattern into the length of the sleeve, you need to know how many rounds the sleeve will have. Your swatch shows that your personal knitting gauge in Rauma Finullgarn is 32 rounds in a 4-inch length. Dividing the number of rounds in the swatch by 4 gives you the number of rounds per inch: 32 (rounds) divided by 4 (inches) = 8 rounds per inch. Now check your paper pattern or the table at right to determine the total length, in inches, you'll need to knit. For size Medium, the table lists 18½ inches as the standard sleeve length above the cuff. Multiply the length by the number of rounds per inch: 18½ (inches) × 8 (rounds per inch) = 148 rounds needed for your sleeve.

Continuing this technique, replace the measurements in italics below with your own numbers or those from the table on page 87; the result is your personalized set of basic instructions.

BODY: Cast on **(circumference at hips × sts/inch)** sts and work ribbing or hem **(length of ribbing or hem)** inches, or longer as desired. Inc evenly to **(circumference above ribbing or hem × sts/inch)** sts.

1. Square neck option: k **(length in front to square neck × rnds/inch)** rnds. Bind off **(width of bind-off at square neck × sts/inch)** sts centered in front of garment. Continue in stockinette st until work measures **(length in back to square neck)** inches. Bind off **(width of bind-off at square neck × sts/inch)** sts centered in back of garment. Continue until work measures **(total length)** inches. Bind off or put all remaining sts on holders.

2. Boat neck option: k (**total length ×
rnds/inch**) rnds. Bind off all sts.

SLEEVES: Cast on (**measurement
around cuff × sts/inch**) sts and work
ribbing or hem (**length of ribbing or
hem**) inches. Then inc evenly to (**circumference above cuff × sts/inch**)
sts. From this point on, you will inc 2
sts per rnd regularly spaced all the way
up the sleeve.

To figure out how often to increase: a)
Subtract (**circumference above cuff ×
sts/inch**) sts from (**circumference at
top of sleeve × sts/inch**) sts. b) Divide
this number by 2. c) Divide the resulting number of sts into (**sleeve length
above cuff × rnds/inch**) rnds. Round
down to the nearest whole number. If
the resulting number is, say, 3, you
must increase 2 sts every third rnd.

Inc 2 sts every (____) rnds until sleeve
measures (**total sleeve length**) or until
you have knitted (**sleeve length above
cuff × rnds/inch**) rnds. Purl one rnd,
then k an inch or so for the sleeve facing. (Note: because they add some
bulk, only make sleeve facings for
sweaters made with sport-weight or
finer yarns.) Bind off, and make another sleeve the same way.

ASSEMBLY AND FINISHING:
Measure the top of the sleeve to determine how large an armhole to make in
the body. Mark this length along the
two side "seams" of the body. With a
sewing machine set to the shortest
stitch length, sew down along one side
of the marked armhole, across 1 or 2
sts, and up along the other side. Make
a second row of machine stitching just
outside the first. Carefully cut the armhole open between the first two lines of
machine stitching. Sew in the sleeves.
To finish a square neck, knit or sew the
shoulders together and sew in the
sleeves (see page 11 for details on these
finishing techniques). To make a neck
facing, use double-pointed needles to
pick up and k one st for every bound
off st at the front and back neck openings, and about 3 sts for every 4 rows
along the side neck edges. Join and k 1
rnd, p 1 rnd, then k ¾ inch, increasing
1 st at each corner in every rnd so that
the facing will lie flat against the inside

of the sweater. Bind off. *To finish a
boat neck,* sew shoulders together on
each side from arm edge toward neck
until neck opening is (**width of boat
neck**) and sew in the sleeves (see page
11 for details on these finishing techniques). To make a neck facing, pick
up and k 1 st for every st along the
front neck opening. Purl 2 rows, then
work stockinette st for ¾ inch and bind
off. Repeat for the back neck facing.
For all sweaters, work in all tails, sew
all hems, and sew down all facings.

If you find these directions compli-
cated, it will help to read through the
directions for the Basic Patterns in the
back of the book. They were put together this way.

*APPLYING CHARTS TO
YOUR BASIC
INSTRUCTIONS*

When you have written out these directions to fit your gauge and measurements, you have instructions for knitting a basic sweater. Now you are ready
to incorporate the multicolored pattern.

The charted pattern should be placed
attractively on the sweater. Its center, if
it has one, should fall exactly at the center stitch of the front, back, and sleeve.
Even if the pattern is tiny and repeated
many times, the center of one motif or
the space separating two motifs should
be aligned with the center stitch. The
human eye is attracted to center lines
and can instantly perceive something
slightly out of line.

If you plan to knit a charted pattern
into the garment, you may find it necessary to adjust the number of stitches in

your garment slightly to fit the pattern
widthwise, but only if you can do so by
adding no more than an inch to the
body circumference or half an inch to
the sleeve circumference. For example,
if the charted pattern is a 10-stitch repeat, the total number of stitches in the
body circumference should be a multiple of 10. You can increase or decrease
the number of rounds too, so that the
vertical repeat in the pattern fits lengthwise. This method is most practical if
you use the same motif throughout and
if there are very few stitches and
rounds in the repeat.

If your charted pattern is too large to
adjust with just a few stitches, you can
use "seam" stitches to break the pattern
where there would be side seams on the
body or an underarm seam on the
sleeve if you were knitting back and
forth on straight needles. Our conven-
tion is to use 2 stitches to mark each of
the side and underarm "seams". (These
"seam" stitches are always worked in
the darkest color used in each round.)
Because the pattern is thus interrupted
at the sides or underarm of the garment, the number of stitches in the pattern needn't fit into the total number of
stitches in the garment evenly.

To center the charted pattern on the
body, start with the total number of
body stitches, for example 200. Divide
this number by 2 to get the number of
stitches in each the front and back:
200/2 = 100. Subtract the 2 stitches
marking the side "seams", one on each
side of the front, and one on each side
of the back. That leaves 98 stitches on
the front for the pattern repeat and 98
stitches on the back. In our example,
the midpoint of the front is between
the forty-ninth and fiftieth stitches. If
your pattern motif is symmetrical
around a center point, you'll need an
odd number of stitches to center the
motif. To get an odd number, add or
subtract 2 stitches from the total number of stitches for the body (one stitch
in front and one stitch in back). For
our example, subtracting 2 stitches will
give a total of 198 stitches, or 99
stitches for each the front and back.
Subtracting 2 stitches for the "seam"
stitches as described above leaves 97

Measurements For All
Standard Sizes

SIZE	½	1	2	3	6	9	12	S	M	L	XL	XXL
SLEEVE												
measurement around cuff	4¼	4¾	4¾	5½	5½	6	6¼	7	7½	8	8¼	8¾
length of ribbing or hem	1¼	1¼	1¼	1¼	2	2	2	2	2	2	2	2
circumference above cuff	6½	6½	8	8	8¾	9½	9½	9½	10	10¾	10¾	13
sleeve length above cuff*	5½	7½	8¾	9½	12	13¾	16½	19	18½	18¼	17¾	17½
total sleeve length*	6¾	8¾	10	10¾	13¾	15¾	18½	21	20½	20	19¾	19¼
circumference at top of sleeve	12½	13¾	15¾	17½	18½	20½	23	23	25¼	26¾	30	31¼
BODY												
circumference at hips	19	20½	22	23	25¼	28	31½	35½	39½	41¾	43½	47¼
length of ribbing or hem	1¼	1¼	1¼	1¼	2	2	2	2	2	2	2	2
circumference above ribbing or hem	20½	23¾	26¾	28¼	30	33	37	41¾	44	47¼	52	56
width of bind-off at boat neck	5½	6½	7½	8	8	8	8	10	10	10	11	11
length in front to square neck	8¼	9½	11	12	13¾	15¾	18½	21¼	21¾	22½	23	23¾
width of bind-off at square neck	3¼	3½	4	4	4	4¼	4¾	5½	5½	5½	6¼	6¼
length in back to square neck edge	9¾	11¼	12½	13¼	15½	17¾	20½	23	23½	24	24¾	25½
total length	10¼	11¾	13	13¾	16	18¼	21	24	24¾	25½	26¼	26¾

*Note: because the instructions are written for drop-shoulder shapings, the sleeve lengths for the larger adult sizes are shorter than the sleeve lengths for the smaller adult sizes.

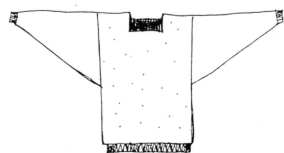

stitches in front on which to center the pattern; stitch number 49 is the center stitch, and there are 48 stitches on each side of it.

Now you're ready to center the charted motif on the body. Begin by dividing the number of stitches in the front (or back) by the number of stitches per pattern repeat to determine how many pattern repeats will fit. For example, if there are 99 stitches in the front (not including "seam" stitches) and the motif repeats every 13 stitches, then there are 99/13 = 7.6 pattern repeats, or 7 full repeats plus 8 stitches left over (7× 13 = 91; 91 + 8 = 99). Divide the number of leftover stitches by 2 to determine the number of extra stitches there will be at each side for the pattern to be centered in the front: 8/2 = 4. (If the number of stitches at this point is not evenly divisible by 2, add or subtract 2 stitches—one for the front and a corresponding one for the back—to the original number of body stitches.) Now count inward from the left edge of the charted pattern 4 stitches to find out where in the motif to begin knitting after the "seam" stitches for both the front and back.

If the charted motif has an even number of stitches per repeat, for example 12, the procedure is the same, but there must be an even number of stitches in the front (and back) on which to center the motif.

The charted pattern is centered on the sleeve in a similar way. Start by dividing the number of stitches above the ribbing or hem by 2. Then subtract the two "seam" stitches. Divide the resulting number by the number of stitches per pattern repeat to determine the number of full repeats and the number of leftover stitches, and then divide the number of leftover stitches by 2. This is the number of stitches to count inward from the left edge of the charted motif, marking where to begin knitting after the "seam" stitches. Keep in mind that as the sleeve increases are made, the pattern motif is expanded symmetrically on both sides of the underarm "seam".

Now try to write directions in a conventional format which are so clear and intelligible that someone else could use them to knit a sweater. If you find this difficult, use one of our completed directions as a model. Add any changes you make to the directions as you knit.

When your sweater is finished, make a clean copy of your corrected directions, slip them into a plastic page protector with a copy of the charted color patterns, and store them in a looseleaf notebook,.

There are many reasons to keep a record of your patterns. Most importantly, you can consult them the next time you want to make a sweater, and avoid repeating mistakes. You can also share the pattern with a friend or even sell the pattern to a yarn company or magazine.

BASIC INSTRUCTIONS

On the following pages you will find basic patterns for the 12 sizes we offer in this book at six different gauges. As always, begin by knitting a tubular test swatch following the charted pattern and using the yarn you plan to use. Count the number of stitches in a 4-inch width and how many rounds in a 4-inch length of the swatch. Adjust your needle size up or down until you like the feel of the knitted swatch and have one of the knitting gauges listed in the basic pattern. Remember that gauge can vary greatly depending on whether you are knitting a structural pattern such as cables, a single color in stocki-

nette stitch, or a two-color pattern—even whether you are knitting back and forth or circularly—so knit your test swatch using the same technique and yarn you plan to use for the garment. Sample knitting gauges are given at the beginning of each basic pattern.

The choice of whether to knit a ribbed edge or a hem is entirely up to you. Most of our patterns have a hem, but you can substitute a ribbed edging if you prefer.

If you are planning a square neckline on a body which has an odd number of stitches in front and in back, the number of stitches you take off for the neck must also be an odd number so that there will be an equal number of stitches on each shoulder. Likewise, if the front and back have an even number of stitches, so must the neckline.

SAMPLE GAUGES FOR DIFFERENT YARNS FOR 4 × 4 INCHES

Heavy worsted-weight wool yarn (such as Rauma Vamsegarn), plain stockinette: 16 sts and 20 rounds.

Heavy worsted-weight wool yarn (such as Rauma Vamsegarn), pattern knitting: 20 sts and 24 rounds.

Light worsted-weight wool yarn (such as Rauma Strikkegarn), plain stockinette: 20 sts and 24 rounds.

Light worsted-weight wool yarn (such as Rauma Strikkegarn), pattern knitting: 24 sts and 28 rounds.

Sport-weight wool yarn (such as Rauma Finullgarn), plain stockinette: 24 sts and 28 rounds.

Sport-weight wool yarn (such as Rauma Finullgarn), pattern knitting: 28 sts and 32 rounds.

Lace-weight wool yarn (such as Rauma Babyull), pattern knitting: 32 sts and 36 rounds.

Figure out which size knitting needle to use by knitting test swatches. Use the garment measurements on page 87 to determine what size garment to knit.

SIZE 6 MONTHS

GAUGE

Sts per 4 inches
16 (20, 24, 28, 32, 36)

Rounds per 4 inches
20 (24, 28, 32, 36, 40)

The numbers above are intended as a starting point. Knit test swatches with the yarn and color pattern you intend to use to determine which of the above gauges gives the fabric you like best. For ribbing use needles two sizes smaller.

SLEEVE: The cuff is 4¼ inches around. With dp needles, cast on 18 (22, 26, 30, 36, 40) sts. Join and work a ribbing (with smaller needles) or a hem for 1¼ inches. If you made a ribbing, change to larger needles in the next row. The sleeve above the cuff is 6½ inches around, so inc evenly to 26 (34, 40, 46, 52, 60) sts. Sleeve length above cuff is 5½ inches, or about 28 (34, 40, 44, 50, 56) rnds. Inc 2 sts every second rnd until you have 50 (64, 76, 88, 100, 114) sts and the measurement around the top of the sleeve is 12½ inches. Continue even until the total sleeve length measures 6¾ inches. If you want a sleeve facing at the top, p 1 rnd, then k 5 rnds. Bind off.

BODY: The sweater is 19 inches around at the hips. With circular needles, cast on 76 (96, 114, 134, 152, 172) sts. Join and work a ribbing (with smaller needles) or hem for 1¼ inches. If you made a ribbing, change to larger needles. Above the ribbing/hem, the sweater should measure 20½ inches around. To get this measurement, inc evenly to 82 (104, 124, 144, 164, 186) sts.

For square neck, work even until body is 8¼ inches long. Bind off 3¼ inches, or 14 (16, 20, 22, 26, 30) sts, at the center front. Work back and forth in stockinette st until body measures 9¾

inches. Bind off the same number of sts at center back as on the front. Continue to work the shoulders separately in stockinette st until body is 10¼ inches long. Bind off shoulder sts for a sewn seam or put on holders for a knitted join. Finish armholes, shoulders, and sleeves as described on page 11. For the neck facing, use dp needles to pick up and k all front and back neck bound-off sts and ⅘ (⅚, 6/7, ⅞, 8/9, 9/10) of all rnds along the sides of the neck. Join and k 1 rnd, p 1 rnd, then k ¾ inch while increasing 1 st in each corner every rnd so that the neck facing will lie flat on the inside. Bind off.

For boat neck, work even until the body is 10¼ inches long. Bind off 22 (28, 34, 38, 44, 50) sts centered on both front and back. Put remaining sts on holders. Finish armholes, shoulders, and sleeves as described on page 11. To make a neck facing, pick up and k all front neck bound-off sts. Purl 2 rows, then work stockinette st for ¾ inch and bind off. Repeat for back neck facing.

FINISHING: Hem the bottom and facings and work all loose ends into the back of the fabric. Lightly steam press.

SIZE 1 YEAR

GAUGE

Sts per 4 inches
16 (20, 24, 28, 32, 36)

Rnds per 4 inches
20 (24, 28, 32, 36, 40)

The numbers above are intended as a starting point. Knit test swatches with the yarn and color pattern you intend to use to determine which of the above gauges gives the fabric you like best. For ribbing use needles two sizes smaller.

SLEEVES: The cuff is 4¾ inches around. With dp needles, cast on 20 (24, 30, 34, 38, 44) sts. Join and work k1, p1 ribbing (with smaller needles) or a hem for 1¼ inch. If you made a ribbing, change to larger needles. The sleeve above the cuff is 6¼ inches around, so inc evenly to 26 (34, 40, 46, 52, 60) sts. Sleeve length above the cuff is 7½ inches, or 38 (44, 53, 60, 68, 75) rnds. The sleeve is 13¾ inches around at the top; inc 2 sts every second rnd until you have 56 (70, 84, 98, 110, 124) sts. Continue even until the total sleeve length measures 8¾ inches. If you wish to make a sleeve facing at the top, p 1 rnd, then k 6 rnds. Bind off.

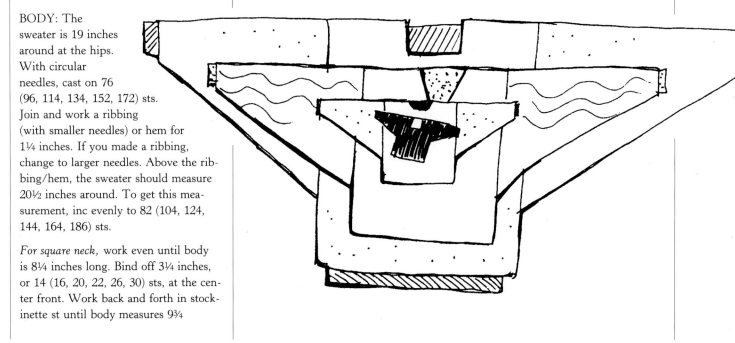

BODY: The sweater is 20½ inches around the hips. With cir needles, cast on 82 (104, 124, 144, 164, 186) sts. Join and work ribbing (with smaller needles) or a hem for 1¼ inches. If you made a ribbing, change to larger needles. The sweater above the ribbing/hem is 23¾ inches around, so inc evenly to 96 (120, 144, 168, 190, 214) sts.

For square neck, work even until body is 9½ inches long. Bind off 3½ inches, or 14 (18, 22, 26, 30, 32) sts, at the center front. Work back and forth in stockinette st until body measures 11¼ inches. Bind off the same number of sts at center back as on the front. Continue to work the shoulders separately in stockinette st until body is 11¾ inches long. Finish armholes, shoulders, and sleeves as described on page 11. For the neck facing, use dp needles to pick up and k all bound-off sts and ⅘ (⅚, 6/7, ⅞, 8/9, 9/10) of all rnds along the sides of the neck. Join and k 1 rnd, p 1 rnd, then k 8 rnds while increasing 1 st in each corner every rnd so that the neck facing will lie flat on the inside.

For boat neck, work even until the body is 11¾ inches long. Bind off 26 (32, 40, 46, 52, 58) sts centered on both front and back. Put remaining sts on holders. Finish armholes, shoulders, and sleeves as described on page 11. To make a neck facing, pick up and k all front neck bound-off sts. Purl 2 rows, then work stockinette st for ¾ inch and bind off. Repeat for back neck facing.

FINISHING: Hem the bottom and facings and work all loose ends into the back of the fabric. Lightly steam press.

SIZE 2 YEARS

GAUGE

Sts per 4 inches
  16 (20, 24, 28, 32, 36)

Rnds per 4 inches
  20 (24, 28, 32, 36, 40)

The numbers above are intended as a starting point. Knit test swatches with the yarn and color pattern you intend to use to determine which of the above gauges gives the fabric you like best. For ribbing use needles two sizes smaller.

SLEEVES: The cuff is 4¾ inches around. With dp needles, cast on 20 (24, 30, 34, 38, 44) sts. Join and work k1, p1 ribbing (with smaller needles) or a hem for 1¼ inch. If you made a ribbing, change to larger needles. The sleeve above the cuff is 8 inches around, so inc evenly to 32 (40, 48, 56, 64, 72) sts. Sleeve length above the cuff is 8¾ inches, or 44 (53, 62, 70, 79, 88) rnds. The sleeve is 15¾ inches around at the top; inc 2 sts every second rnd until you have 64 (80, 96, 112, 126, 142) sts. Continue even until the total sleeve length measures 10 inches. If you wish to make a sleeve facing at the top, p 1 rnd, then k 6 rnds. Bind off.

BODY: The sweater is 22 inches around the hips. With cir needles, cast on 88 (110, 132, 154, 176, 198) sts. Join and work ribbing (with smaller needles) or a hem for 1¼ inches. If you made a ribbing, change to larger needles. The sweater above the ribbing/hem is 26¾ inches around, so inc evenly to 108 (134, 162, 188, 214, 242) sts.

For square neck, work even until body is 11 inches long. Bind off 4 inches, or 16 (20, 24, 28, 32, 36) sts, at the center front. Work back and forth in stockinette st until body measures 12½ inches. Bind off the same number of sts at center back as on the front. Continue to work the shoulders separately in stockinette st until body is 13 inches long. Finish armholes, shoulders, and

---

sleeves as described on page 11. For the neck facing, use dp needles to pick up and k all bound-off sts and ⅘ (⅚, 6/7, ⅞, 8/9, 9/10) of all rnds along the sides of the neck. Join and k 1 rnd, p 1 rnd, then k 8 rnds while increasing 1 st in each corner every rnd so that the neck facing will lie flat on the inside.

For boat neck, work even until the body is 13 inches long. Bind off 30 (38, 46, 52, 60, 68) sts centered on both front and back. Put remaining sts on holders. Finish armholes, shoulders, and sleeves as described on page 11. To make a neck facing, pick up and k all front neck bound-off sts. Purl 2 rows, then work stockinette st for ¾ inch and bind off. Repeat for back neck facing.

FINISHING: Hem the bottom and facings and work all loose ends into the back of the fabric. Lightly steam press.

SIZE 3 YEARS

GAUGE

Sts per 4 inches
16 (20, 24, 28, 32, 36)

Rnds per 4 inches
20 (24, 28, 32, 36, 40)

The numbers above are intended as a starting point. Knit test swatches with the yarn and color pattern you intend to use to determine which of the above gauges gives the fabric you like best. For ribbing use needles two sizes smaller.

SLEEVES: The cuff is 5½ inches around. With dp needles, cast on 22 (28, 34, 40, 44, 50) sts. Join and work k1, p1 ribbing (with smaller needles) or a hem for 1¼ inch. If you made a ribbing, change to larger needles. The sleeve above the cuff is 8 inches around, so inc evenly to 32 (40, 48, 56, 64, 72) sts. Sleeve length above the cuff is 9½ inches, or 48 (57, 67, 76, 86, 95) rnds. The sleeve is 17½ inches around at the top; inc 2 sts every second rnd until you have 70 (88, 106, 124, 140, 158) sts. Continue even until the total sleeve length measures 10 inches. If you wish to make a sleeve facing at the top, p 1 rnd, then k 6 rnds. Bind off.

BODY: The sweater is 23 inches around the hips. With cir needles, cast on 92 (116, 138, 162, 184, 208) sts. Join and work ribbing (with smaller needles) or a hem for 1¼ inches. If you made a ribbing, change to larger needles. The sweater above the ribbing/hem is 28¼ inches around, so inc evenly to 114 (142, 170, 198, 226, 254) sts.

For square neck, work even until body is 12 inches long. Bind off 4 inches, or 16 (20, 24, 28, 32, 36) sts, at the center front. Work back and forth in stockinette st until body measures 13¼ inches. Bind off the same number of sts at center back as on the front. Continue to work the shoulders separately in stockinette st until body is 13¾ inches long. Finish armholes, shoulders, and

sleeves as described on page 11. For the neck facing, use dp needles to pick up and k all bound-off sts and ⅘ (⅚, ⁶⁄₇, ⅞, ⁸⁄₉, ⁹⁄₁₀) of all rnds along the sides of the neck. Join and k 1 rnd, p 1 rnd, then k 8 rnds while increasing 1 st in each corner every rnd so that the neck facing will lie flat on the inside.

For boat neck, work even until the body is 13¾ inches long. Bind off 32 (40, 48, 56, 64, 72) sts centered on both front and back. Put remaining sts on holders. Finish armholes, shoulders, and sleeves as described on page 11. To make a neck facing, pick up and k all front neck bound-off sts. Purl 2 rows, then work stockinette st for ¾ inch and bind off. Repeat for back neck facing.

FINISHING: Hem the bottom and facings and work all loose ends into the back of the fabric. Lightly steam press.

SIZE 6 YEARS

GAUGE

Sts per 4 inches
16 (20, 24, 28, 32, 36)

Rnds per 4 inches
20 (24, 28, 32, 36, 40)

The numbers above are intended as a starting point. Knit test swatches with the yarn and color pattern you intend to use to determine which of the above gauges gives the fabric you like best. For ribbing use needles two sizes smaller.

SLEEVES: The cuff is 5½ inches around. With dp needles, cast on 22 (28, 34, 40, 44, 50) sts. Join and work k1, p1 ribbing (with smaller needles) or a hem for 2 inches. If you made a ribbing, change to larger needles. The sleeve above the cuff is 8¾ inches around, so inc evenly to 36 (44, 54, 62, 70, 80) sts. Sleeve length above the cuff is 12 inches, or 60 (72, 84, 96, 108, 120) rnds. The sleeve is 18½ inches around at the top; inc 2 sts every second rnd until you have 74 (94, 112, 130, 148, 168) sts. Continue even until the total sleeve length measures 13¾ inches. If you wish to make a sleeve facing at the top, p 1 rnd, then k 6 rnds. Bind off.

BODY: The sweater is 25¼ inches around the hips. With cir needles, cast on 102 (128, 152, 178, 202, 228) sts. Join and work ribbing (with smaller needles) or a hem for 2 inches. If you made a ribbing, change to larger needles. The sweater above the ribbing/hem is 30 inches around, so inc evenly to 120 (152, 180, 210, 240, 270) sts.

For square neck, work even until body is 13¾ inches long. Bind off 4 inches, or 16 (20, 24, 28, 32, 36) sts, at the center front. Work back and forth in stockinette st until body measures 15½ inches. Bind off the same number of sts at center back as on the front. Continue to work the shoulders separately in stockinette st until body is 16 inches long. Finish armholes, shoulders, and sleeves as described on page 11. For the neck facing, use dp needles to pick up and k all bound-off sts and $\frac{4}{5}$ ($\frac{5}{6}$, $\frac{6}{7}$, $\frac{7}{8}$, $\frac{8}{9}$, $\frac{9}{10}$) of all rnds along the sides of the neck. Join and k 1 rnd, p 1 rnd, then k 8 rnds while increasing 1 st in each corner every rnd so that the neck facing will lie flat on the inside.

For boat neck, work even until the body is 16 inches long. Bind off 32 (40, 48, 56, 64, 72) sts centered on both front and back. Put remaining sts on holders. Finish armholes, shoulders, and sleeves as described on page 11. To make a neck facing, pick up and k all front neck bound-off sts. Purl 2 rows, then work stockinette st for $\frac{3}{4}$ inch and bind off. Repeat for back neck facing.

FINISHING: Hem the bottom and facings and work all loose ends into the back of the fabric. Lightly steam press.

BASIC INSTRUCTIONS

SIZE 9 YEARS

GAUGE

Sts per 4 inches
   16 (20, 24, 28, 32, 36)

Rnds per 4 inches
   20, (24, 28, 32, 36, 40)

The numbers above are intended as a starting point. Knit test swatches with the yarn and color pattern you intend to use to determine which of the above gauges gives the fabric you like best. For ribbing use needles two sizes smaller.

SLEEVES: The cuff is 6 inches around. With dp needles, cast on 24 (30, 36, 42, 48, 54) sts. Join and work k1, p1 ribbing (with smaller needles) or a hem for 2 inches. If you made a ribbing, change to larger needles. The sleeve above the cuff is 9½ inches around, so inc evenly to 38 (48, 58, 68, 76, 86) sts. Sleeve length above the cuff is 13¾ inches, or 70 (84, 98, 110, 124, 138) rnds. The sleeve is 20½ inches around at the top; inc 2 sts every third (third, third, second, second, second) rnd until you have 82 (104, 124, 144, 164, 186) sts. Continue even until the total sleeve length measures 15¾ inches. If you wish to make a sleeve facing at the top, p 1 rnd, then k 6 rnds. Bind off.

BODY: The sweater is 28 inches around the hips. With cir needles, cast on 112 (140, 168, 196, 224, 252) sts. Join and work ribbing (with smaller needles) or a hem for 2 inches. If you made a ribbing, change to larger needles. The sweater above the ribbing/hem is 33 inches around, so inc evenly to 132 (166, 198, 232, 264, 298) sts.

For square neck, work even until body is 15¾ inches long. Bind off 4¼ inches, or 18 (22, 26, 30, 34, 40) sts, at the center front. Work back and forth in stockinette st until body measures 17¾ inches. Bind off the same number of sts at center back as on the front. Continue to work the shoulders separately in stockinette st until body is 18¼ inches

---

long. Finish armholes, shoulders, and sleeves as described on page 11. For the neck facing, use dp needles to pick up and k all bound-off sts and $\frac{4}{5}$ ($\frac{5}{6}$, $\frac{6}{7}$, $\frac{7}{8}$, $\frac{8}{9}$, $\frac{9}{10}$) of all rnds along the sides of the neck. Join and k 1 rnd, p 1 rnd, then k 8 rnds while increasing 1 st in each corner every rnd so that the neck facing will lie flat on the inside.

For boat neck, work even until the body is 16 inches long. Bind off 32 (40, 48, 56, 64, 72) sts centered on both front and back. Put remaining sts on holders. Finish armholes, shoulders, and sleeves as described on page 11. To make a neck facing, pick up and k all front neck bound-off sts. Purl 2 rows, then work stockinette st for $\frac{3}{4}$ inch and bind off. Repeat for back neck facing.

FINISHING: Hem the bottom and facings and work all loose ends into the back of the fabric. Lightly steam press.

SIZE 12 YEARS

GAUGE

Sts per 4 inches
16 (20, 24, 28, 32, 36)

Rnds per 4 inches
20 (24, 28, 32, 36, 40)

The numbers above are intended as a starting point. Knit test swatches with the yarn and color pattern you intend to use to determine which of the above gauges gives the fabric you like best. For ribbing use needles two sizes smaller.

SLEEVES: The cuff is 6¼ inches around. With dp needles, cast on 26 (32, 38, 44, 50, 58) sts. Join and work k1, p1 ribbing (with smaller needles) or a hem for 2 inches. If you made a ribbing, change to larger needles. The sleeve above the cuff is 9½ inches around, so inc evenly to 38 (48, 58, 68, 76, 86) sts. Sleeve length above the cuff is 16½ inches, or 83 (99, 116, 132, 149, 166) rnds. The sleeve is 23 inches around at the top; inc 2 sts every second rnd until you have 92 (116, 138, 162, 184, 208) sts. Continue even until the total sleeve length measures 18½ inches. If you wish to make a sleeve facing at the top, p 1 rnd, then k 6 rnds. Bind off.

BODY: The sweater is 31½ inches around the hips. With cir needles, cast on 126 (158, 190, 222, 252, 284) sts. Join and work ribbing (with smaller needles) or a hem for 2 inches. If you made a ribbing, change to larger needles. The sweater above the ribbing/hem is 37 inches around, so inc evenly to 148 (186, 222, 260, 296, 334) sts.

For square neck, work even until body is 18½ inches long. Bind off 4¾ inches, or 20 (24, 30, 34, 38, 44) sts, at the center front. Work back and forth in stockinette st until body measures 20½ inches. Bind off the same number of sts at center back as on the front. Continue to work the shoulders separately in stockinette st until body is 21 inches

long. Finish armholes, shoulders, and sleeves as described on page 11. For the neck facing, use dp needles to pick up and k all bound-off sts and ⅘ (⅚, ⁶⁄₇, ⅞, ⁸⁄₉, ⁹⁄₁₀) of all rnds along the sides of the neck. Join and k 1 rnd, p 1 rnd, then k 8 rnds while increasing 1 st in each corner every rnd so that the neck facing will lie flat on the inside.

For boat neck, work even until the body is 21 inches long. Bind off 32 (40, 48, 56, 64, 72) sts centered on both front and back. Put remaining sts on holders. Finish armholes, shoulders, and sleeves as described on page 11. To make a neck facing, pick up and k all front neck bound-off sts. Purl 2 rows, then work stockinette st for ¾ inch and bind off. Repeat for back neck facing.

FINISHING: Hem the bottom and facings and work all loose ends into the back of the fabric. Lightly steam press.

ADULT SIZE SMALL

GAUGE

Sts per 4 inches
16 (20, 24, 28, 32, 36)

Rnds per 4 inches
20 (24, 28, 32, 36, 40)

The numbers above are intended as a starting point. Knit test swatches with the yarn and color pattern you intend to use to determine which of the above gauges gives the fabric you like best. For ribbing use needles two sizes smaller.

SLEEVES: The cuff is 7 inches around. With dp needles, cast on 28 (36, 42, 50, 56, 64) sts. Join and work k1, p1 ribbing (with smaller needles) or a hem for 2 inches. If you made a ribbing, change to larger needles. The sleeve above the cuff is 9½ inches around, so inc evenly to 38 (48, 58, 68, 76, 86) sts. Sleeve length above the cuff is 19 inches, or 95 (114, 133, 152, 171, 190) rnds. The sleeve is 23 inches around at the top; inc 2 sts every third rnd until you have 92 (116, 138, 162, 184, 208) sts. Continue even until the total sleeve length measures 21 inches. If you wish to make a sleeve facing at the top, p 1 rnd, then k 6 rnds. Bind off.

BODY: The sweater is 35½ inches around the hips. With cir needles, cast on 142 (178, 214, 250, 284, 320) sts. Join and work ribbing (with smaller needles) or a hem for 2 inches. If you made a ribbing, change to larger needles. The sweater above the ribbing/hem is 41¾ inches around, so inc evenly to 168 (210, 252, 294, 334, 376) sts.

For square neck, work even until body is 21¼ inches long. Bind off 5½ inches, or 22 (28, 34, 40, 44, 50) sts, at the center front. Work back and forth in stockinette st until body measures 23 inches. Bind off the same number of sts at center back as on the front. Continue to work the shoulders separately in stockinette st until body is 24 inches long. Finish armholes, shoulders, and sleeves as described on page 11. For the neck facing, use dp needles to pick up and k all bound-off sts and ⅘ (⅚, ⁶⁄₇, ⅞, ⁸⁄₉, ⁹⁄₁₀) of all rnds along the sides of the neck. Join and k 1 rnd, p 1 rnd, then k 8 rnds while increasing 1 st in each corner every rnd so that the neck facing will lie flat on the inside.

For boat neck, work even until the body is 24 inches long. Bind off 40 (50, 60, 70, 80, 90) sts centered on both front and back. Put remaining sts on holders. Finish armholes, shoulders, and sleeves as described on page 11. To make a neck facing, pick up and k all front neck bound-off sts. Purl 2 rows, then work stockinette st for ¾ inch and bind off. Repeat for back neck facing.

FINISHING: Hem the bottom and facings and work all loose ends into the back of the fabric. Lightly steam press.

ADULT SIZE MEDIUM

GAUGE

Sts per 4 inches
    16 (20, 24, 28, 32, 36)

Rnds per 4 inches
    20 (24, 28, 32, 36, 40)

The numbers above are intended as a starting point. Knit test swatches with the yarn and color pattern you intend to use to determine which of the above gauges gives the fabric you like best. For ribbing use needles two sizes smaller.

SLEEVES: The cuff is 7½ inches around. With dp needles, cast on 30 (38, 46, 54, 60, 68) sts. Join and work k1, p1 ribbing (with smaller needles) or a hem for 2 inches. If you made a ribbing, change to larger needles. The sleeve above the cuff is 10 inches around, so inc evenly to 40 (50, 60, 70, 80, 90) sts. Sleeve length above the cuff is 18½ inches, or 93 (111, 130, 148, 167, 185) rnds. The sleeve is 23 inches around at the top; inc 2 sts every second rnd until you have 102 (128, 152, 178, 202, 228) sts. Continue even until the total sleeve length measures 20½ inches. If you wish to make a sleeve facing at the top, p 1 rnd, then k 8 rnds. Bind off.

BODY: The sweater is 39½ inches around the hips. With cir needles, cast on 158 (198, 238, 278, 316, 356) sts. Join and work ribbing (with smaller needles) or a hem for 2 inches. If you made a ribbing, change to larger needles. The sweater above the ribbing/hem is 44 inches around, so inc evenly to 176 (220, 264, 308, 352, 396) sts.

For square neck, work even until body is 21¾ inches long. Bind off 5½ inches, or 22 (28, 34, 40, 44, 50) sts, at the center front. Work back and forth in stockinette st until body measures 23½ inches. Bind off the same number of sts at center back as on the front. Continue to work the shoulders separately in stockinette st until body is 24¾ inches

long. Finish armholes, shoulders, and sleeves as described on page 11. For the neck facing, use dp needles to pick up and k all bound-off sts and ⅘ (⅚, ⁶⁄₇, ⅞, ⁸⁄₉, ⁹⁄₁₀) of all rnds along the sides of the neck. Join and k 1 rnd, p 1 rnd, then k 8 rnds while increasing 1 st in each corner every rnd so that the neck facing will lie flat on the inside.

For boat neck, work even until the body is 24¾ inches long. Bind off 40 (50, 60, 70, 80, 90) sts centered on both front and back. Put remaining sts on holders. Finish armholes, shoulders, and sleeves as described on page 11. To make a neck facing, pick up and k all front neck bound-off sts. Purl 2 rows, then work stockinette st for ¾ inch and bind off. Repeat for back neck facing.

FINISHING: Hem the bottom and facings and work all loose ends into the back of the fabric. Lightly steam press.

ADULT SIZE LARGE

GAUGE

Sts per 4 inches
16 (20, 24, 28, 32, 36)

Rnds per 4 inches
20 (24, 28, 32, 36, 40)

The numbers above are intended as a starting point. Knit test swatches with the yarn and color pattern you intend to use to determine which of the above gauges gives the fabric you like best. For ribbing use needles two sizes smaller.

SLEEVES: The cuff is 8 inches around. With dp needles, cast on 32 (40, 48, 56, 64, 72) sts. Join and work k1, p1 ribbing (with smaller needles) or a hem for 2 inches. If you made a ribbing, change to larger needles. The sleeve above the cuff is 10¾ inches around, so inc evenly to 44 (54, 66, 76, 86, 98) sts. Sleeve length above the cuff is 18¼ inches, or 92 (110, 128, 146, 165, 183) rnds. The sleeve is 26¾ inches around at the top; inc 2 sts every second rnd until you have 108 (134, 162, 188, 214, 242) sts. Continue even until the total sleeve length measures 20 inches. If you wish to make a sleeve facing at the top, p 1 rnd, then k 8 rnds. Bind off.

BODY: The sweater is 41¾ inches around the hips. With cir needles, cast on 168 (210, 252, 294, 334, 376) sts. Join and work ribbing (with smaller needles) or a hem for 2 inches. If you made a ribbing, change to larger needles. The sweater above the ribbing/hem is 47¼ inches around, so inc evenly to 190 (238, 284, 332, 378, 426) sts.

For square neck, work even until body is 22½ inches long. Bind off 5½ inches, or 22 (28, 34, 40, 44, 50) sts, at the center front. Work back and forth in stockinette st until body measures 24 inches. Bind off the same number of sts at center back as on the front. Continue to work the shoulders separately in stockinette st until body is 25½ inches long. Finish armholes, shoulders, and sleeves as described on page 11. For the neck facing, use dp needles to pick up and k all bound-off sts and ⅘ (⅚, ⁶⁄₇, ⅞, ⁸⁄₉, ⁹⁄₁₀) of all rnds along the sides of the neck. Join and k 1 rnd, p 1 rnd, then k 8 rnds while increasing 1 st in each corner every rnd so that the neck facing will lie flat on the inside.

For boat neck, work even until the body is 25½ inches long. Bind off 40 (50, 60, 70, 80, 90) sts centered on both front and back. Put remaining sts on holders. Finish armholes, shoulders, and sleeves as described on page 11. To make a neck facing, pick up and k all front neck bound-off sts. Purl 2 rows, then work stockinette st for ¾ inch and bind off. Repeat for back neck facing.

FINISHING: Hem the bottom and facings and work all loose ends into the back of the fabric. Lightly steam press.

ADULT SIZE EXTRA-LARGE

GAUGE

Sts per 4 inches
16 (20, 24, 28, 32, 36)

Rnds per 4 inches
20 (24, 28, 32, 36, 40)

The numbers above are intended as a starting point. Knit test swatches with the yarn and color pattern you intend to use to determine which of the above gauges gives the fabric you like best. For ribbing use needles two sizes smaller.

SLEEVES: The cuff is 8¼ inches around. With dp needles, cast on 34 (42, 50, 58, 66, 76) sts. Join and work k1, p1 ribbing (with smaller needles) or a hem for 2 inches. If you made a ribbing, change to larger needles. The sleeve above the cuff is 10¾ inches around, so inc evenly to 44 (54, 66, 76, 86, 98) sts. Sleeve length above the cuff is 17¾ inches, or 89 (107, 125, 142, 160, 178) rnds. The sleeve is 30 inches around at the top; inc 2 sts every second rnd until you have 120 (150, 180, 210, 240, 270) sts. Continue even until the total sleeve length measures 19¾ inches. If you wish to make a sleeve facing at the top, p 1 rnd, then k 8 rnds. Bind off.

BODY: The sweater is 43½ inches around the hips. With cir needles, cast on 174 (218, 262, 306, 348, 392) sts. Join and work ribbing (with smaller needles) or a hem for 2 inches. If you made a ribbing, change to larger needles. The sweater above the ribbing/hem is 52 inches around, so inc evenly to 208 (260, 312, 364, 416, 468) sts.

For square neck, work even until body is 23 inches long. Bind off 6¼ inches, or 26 (32, 38, 44, 50, 58) sts, at the center front. Work back and forth in stockinette st until body measures 24¾ inches. Bind off the same number of sts at center back as on the front. Continue to work the shoulders separately in stockinette st until body is 26¼ inches long. Finish armholes, shoulders, and sleeves as described on page 11. For the neck facing, use dp needles to pick up and k all bound-off sts and ⅘ (⅚, ⁶⁄₇, ⅞, ⁸⁄₉, ⁹⁄₁₀) of all rnds along the sides of the neck. Join and k 1 rnd, p 1 rnd, then k 8 rnds while increasing 1 st in each corner every rnd so that the neck facing will lie flat on the inside.

For boat neck, work even until the body is 26¼ inches long. Bind off 44 (56, 66, 78, 88, 100) sts centered on both front and back. Put remaining sts on holders. Finish armholes, shoulders, and sleeves as described on page 11. To make a neck facing, pick up and k all front neck bound-off sts. Purl 2 rows, then work stockinette st for ¾ inch and bind off. Repeat for back neck facing.

FINISHING: Hem the bottom and facings and work all loose ends into the back of the fabric. Lightly steam press.

BASIC INSTRUCTIONS

ADULT SIZE EXTRA-EXTRA-LARGE

GAUGE

Sts per 4 inches
  16 (20, 24, 28, 32, 36)

Rnds per 4 inches
  20 (24, 28, 32, 36, 40)

The numbers above are intended as a starting point. Knit test swatches with the yarn and color pattern you intend to use to determine which of the above gauges gives the fabric you like best. For ribbing use needles two sizes smaller.

SLEEVES: The cuff is 8¾ inches around. With dp needles, cast on 36 (44, 54, 62, 70, 80) sts. Join and work k1, p1 ribbing (with smaller needles) or a hem for 2 inches. If you made a ribbing, change to larger needles. The sleeve above the cuff is 13 inches around, so inc evenly to 52 (66, 78, 92, 104, 118) sts. Sleeve length above the cuff is 17½ inches, or 88 (106, 123, 140, 158, 175) rnds. The sleeve is 31¼ inches around at the top; inc 2 sts every second rnd until you have 126 (158, 188, 220, 250, 282) sts. Continue even until the total sleeve length measures 19¼ inches. If you wish to make a sleeve facing at the top, p 1 rnd, then k 8 rnds. Bind off.

BODY: The sweater is 47¼ inches around the hips. With cir needles, cast on 190 (238, 284, 332, 378, 426) sts. Join and work ribbing (with smaller needles) or a hem for 2 inches. If you made a ribbing, change to larger needles. The sweater above the ribbing/hem is 56 inches around, so inc evenly to 224 (288, 336, 392, 448, 504) sts.

For square neck, work even until body is 23¾ inches long. Bind off 6¼ inches, or 26 (32, 38, 44, 50, 58) sts, at the center front. Work back and forth in stockinette st until body measures 25½ inches. Bind off the same number of sts at center back as on the front. Continue to work the shoulders separately in stockinette st until body is 26¾ inches long. Finish armholes, shoulders, and sleeves as described on page 11. For the neck facing, use dp needles to pick up and k all bound-off sts and ⅘ (⅚, ⁶⁄₇, ⅞, ⁸⁄₉, ⁹⁄₁₀) of all rnds along the sides of the neck. Join and k 1 rnd, p 1 rnd, then k 8 rnds while increasing 1 st in each corner every rnd so that the neck facing will lie flat on the inside.

For boat neck, work even until the body is 26¾ inches long. Bind off 44 (56, 66, 78, 88, 100) sts centered on both front and back. Put remaining sts on holders. Finish armholes, shoulders, and sleeves as described on page 11. To make a neck facing, pick up and k all front neck bound-off sts. Purl 2 rows, then work stockinette st for ¾ inch and bind off. Repeat for back neck facing.

FINISHING: Hem the bottom and facings and work all loose ends into the back of the fabric. Lightly steam press.

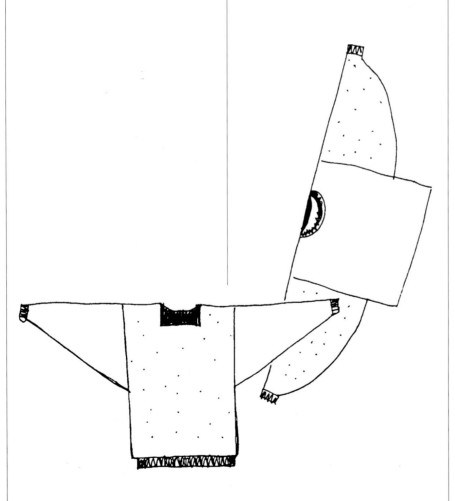

DESIGN 1

GREEN-SLEEVES PULLOVER

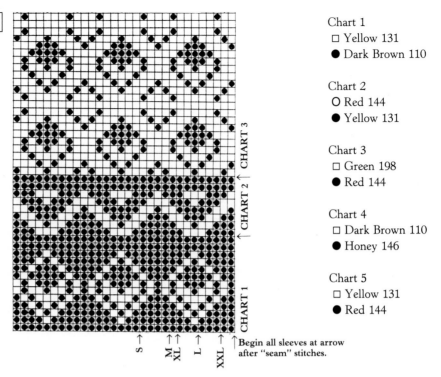

Chart 1
□ Yellow 131
● Dark Brown 110

Chart 2
○ Red 144
● Yellow 131

Chart 3
□ Green 198
● Red 144

Chart 4
□ Dark Brown 110
● Honey 146

Chart 5
□ Yellow 131
● Red 144

Begin all sleeves at arrow after "seam" stitches.

Begin body at arrow for your size after "seam" stitches.

S   M   XL   L   XXL

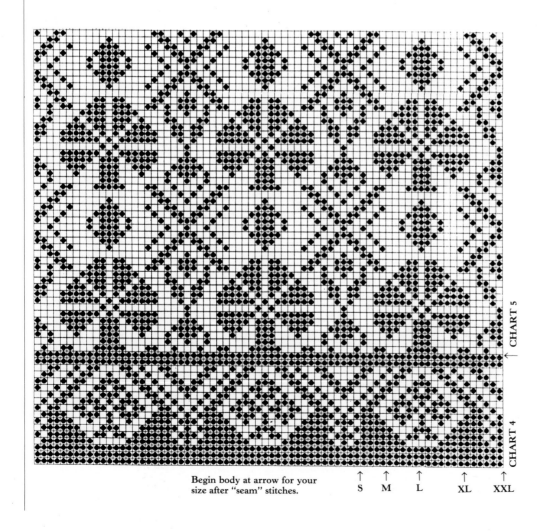

Begin body at arrow for your size after "seam" stitches.

S   M   L   XL   XXL

RED STARS PULLOVER

Chart 1
□ Scarlet 124
● Burgundy 180/Red Brown 127

Chart 2
□ Scarlet 124
● Maroon 128

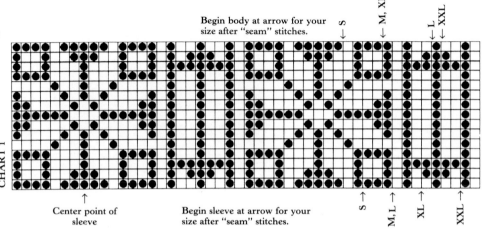

Begin body at arrow for your size after "seam" stitches.

CHART 1

↑ Center point of sleeve

Begin sleeve at arrow for your size after "seam" stitches.

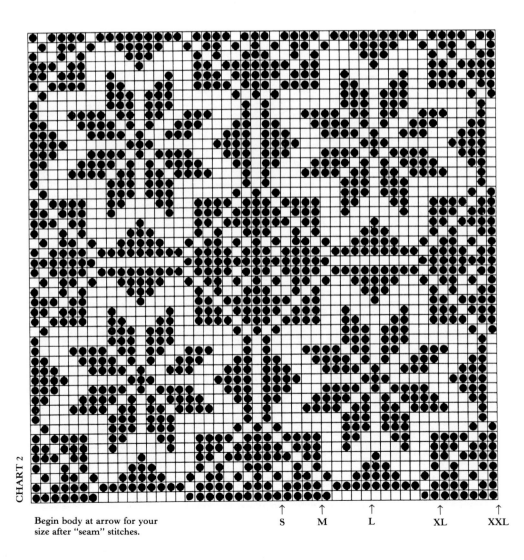

CHART 2

Begin body at arrow for your size after "seam" stitches.

S   M   L   XL   XXL

STARS AND
FLOWERS
FOR A
CHILD

Chart 1
□ Mustard 150
● Dark Blue 143

Chart 2
□ Honey 146
● Midnight Blue 167

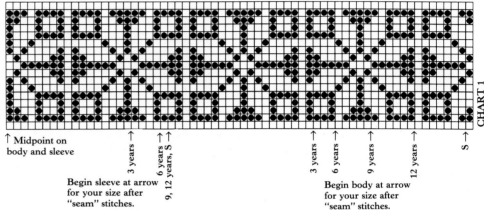

↑ Midpoint on
body and sleeve

3 years →
6 years →
9, 12 years, S →

Begin sleeve at arrow
for your size after
"seam" stitches.

3 years →
6 years →
9 years →
12 years →

S →

Begin body at arrow
for your size after
"seam" stitches.

CHART 1

Begin sleeve at arrow
for your size after
"seam" stitches.

3 years →
6 years →
9, 12 years, S →

Begin body at arrow
for your size after
"seam" stitches.

3 years →
6 years →
9 years →
12 years →

S →

CHART 2

REDBIRD PULLOVER

Chart 1
□ Turquoise 483
● Rust 434

Chart 2
□ Light Burgundy 499 (sleeve), Burgundy 480 (body)
● Burgundy 480 (sleeve), Light Burgundy 499 (body)

Chart 3
□ Light Burgundy 499 (sleeve), Burgundy 480 (body)
● Burgundy 480 (sleeve), Light Burgundy 499 (body)

Chart 4
□ Turquoise 483
● Light Burgundy 499
○ Burgundy 480

Chart 5
□ Turquoise 483
● Burgundy 480

Chart 6
□ Light Burgundy 499 (sleeve), Turquoise 483 (body)
● Rust 434

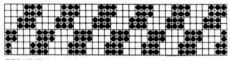

CHART 1

CHART 6

Begin body at arrow for your size after "seam" stitches.

S   M   L   XL

Begin here for sleeve.

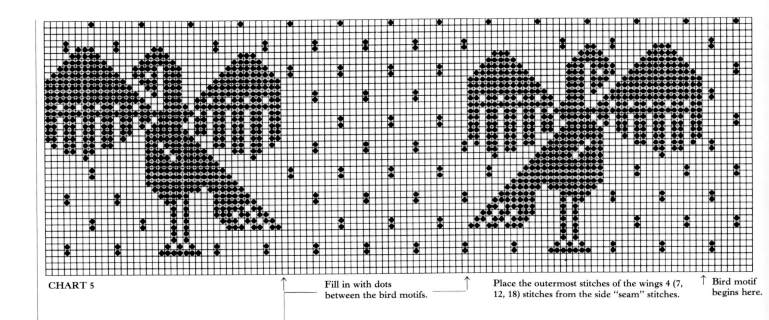

CHART 5

↑ Bird motif begins here.

Fill in with dots between the bird motifs.

↑ Place the outermost stitches of the wings 4 (7, 12, 18) stitches from the side "seam" stitches.

↑ Bird motif begins here.

DESIGN 5

IRON GATE PULLOVER

Chart 1
- □ Turquoise V83
- ● Burgundy V19

Chart 2
- □ Yellow V46
- ● Dark Lilac V81

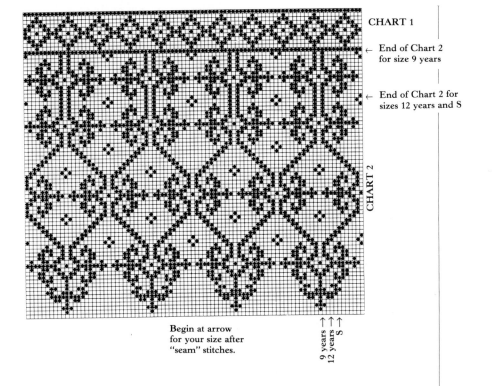

CHART 1

← End of Chart 2 for size 9 years

← End of Chart 2 for sizes 12 years and S

CHART 2

Begin at arrow for your size after "seam" stitches.

↑ 9 years
↑ 12 years
↑ S

CHART 1

DESIGN 6

AUTUMN
POINSETTIAS
JACKET

Chart 1
☐ Dark Lilac 470
● Yellow Green 498
○ Dark Rust 428
◨ Light Rust 434

Chart 2
☐ Dark Lilac 470 (sleeve), Dark Rust 428 (body)
● Dark Rust 428 (sleeve), Dark Lilac 470 (body)

Chart 3
☐ Yellow Green 498
◨ Light Rust 434
○ Dark Rust 428
● Dark Lilac 470

Chart 4
☐ Dark Lilac 470
● Dark Rust 428
○ Light Rust 434
⊠ Medium Rust 419

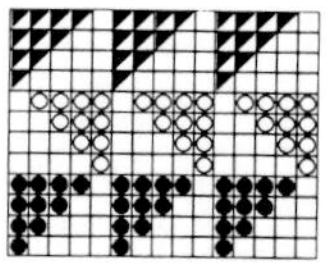

CHART 3

CHART 2

Begin body at arrow for your size after "seam" stitches.

↑ ↑ ↑ ↑
XXL XL L M

↑ Begin all sleeves at arrow after "seam" stitches.

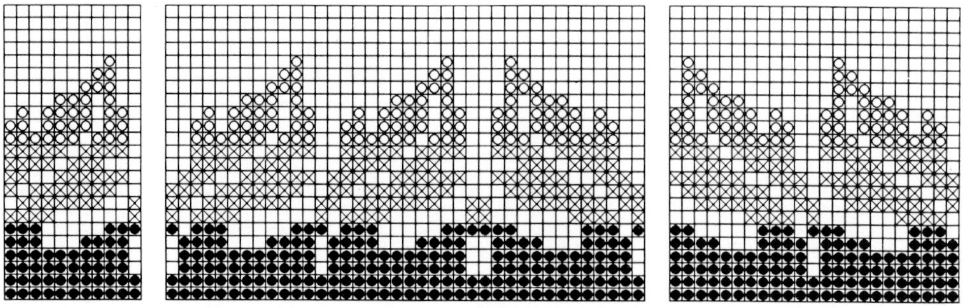

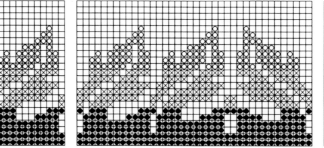

↑ Midpoint of back; change the direction of the leaves.

↑ Begin here. Number of sts must be divisible by 12.

CHART 4

RUST DAMASK JACKET

Chart 1
- □ Medium Rust 419
- ● Deep Rust 444

Chart 2
- □ Gray 4287
- ● Light Rust 434
- ○ Medium Rust 419

CHART 1

Begin body and ↑
sleeve at arrow
for your size after
"seam" stitches.

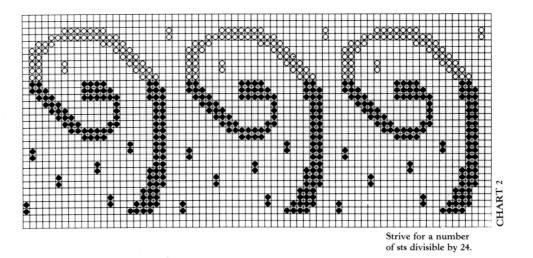

CHART 2

Strive for a number
of sts divisible by 24.

CHILD'S
REDBIRD
PULLOVER

Chart 1 (Version A)
□ Yellow 431
● Lavender 4088
O Dark Pink 465

Chart 2 (Version A)
□ Yellow 431
● Red 439

Chart 1 (Version B)
□ Green 455
■ Pink 479
O Scarlet 424

Chart 2 (Version B)
□ Green 455
● Cyclamen 4886

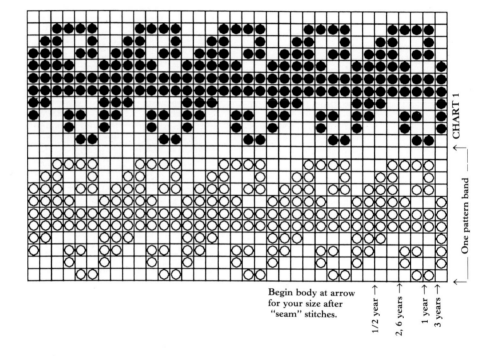

Begin body at arrow for your size after "seam" stitches.

1/2 year →
2, 6 years →
1 year →
3 years →

CHART 1

← One pattern band —

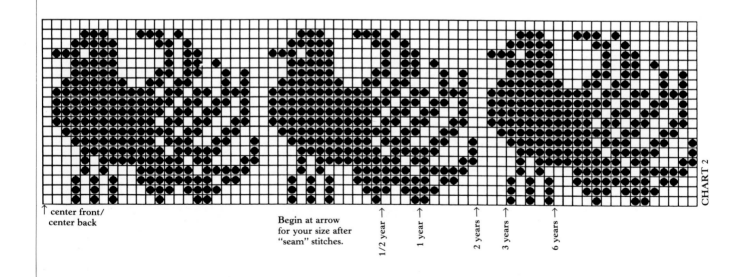

↑ center front/
center back

Begin at arrow for your size after "seam" stitches.

1/2 year →
1 year →
2 years →
3 years →
6 years →

CHART 2

FLOWER TRELLIS PULLOVER

Chart 1
☐ Medium Green 458
● Red 418

Chart 2
☐ Yellow 412
● Red 418

Chart 3
☐ Apple Green 454 (sleeve),
Dark Green 432 (body)
● Medium Green 458 (sleeve),
Red 418 (body)

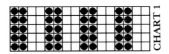

CHART 1

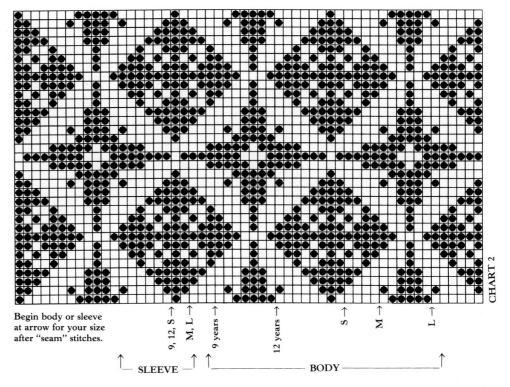

CHART 2

Begin body or sleeve
at arrow for your size
after "seam" stitches.

9, 12, S →
M, L →
9 years →
12 years →
S →
M →
L →

↑ └─ SLEEVE ─┘ ↑ └──────── BODY ────────┘ ↑

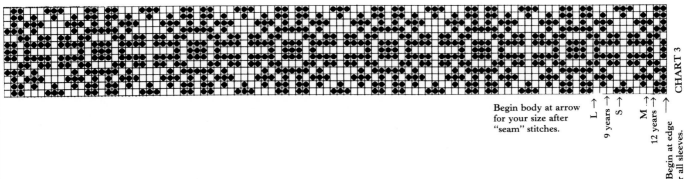

CHART 3

Begin body at arrow
for your size after
"seam" stitches.

L →
9 years →
S →
M →
12 years →

Begin at edge
for all sleeves. →

Chart 4
☐ Yellow 412
● Red 418

Chart 5
☐ Yellow 412
● Red 418

Knit the flower pattern
only on the front.

On the back, knit the
diamonds throughout.

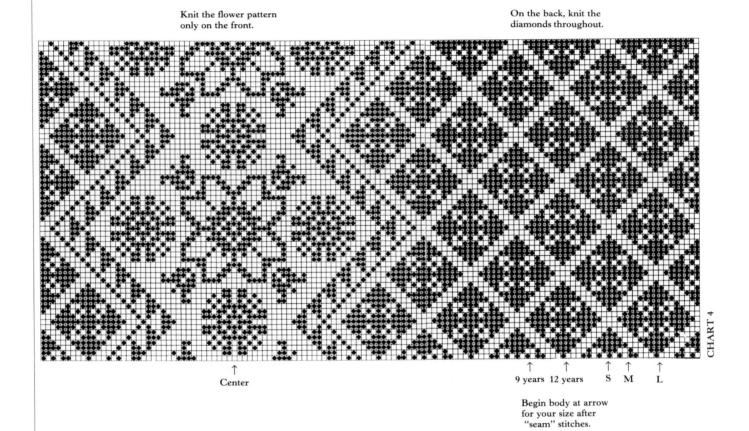

Center

9 years 12 years   S   M   L

Begin body at arrow
for your size after
"seam" stitches.

CHART 4

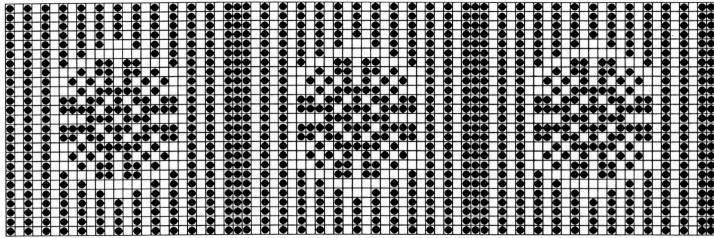

CHART 5

DESIGN 10

BLOOMING CYCLAMEN PULLOVER

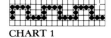

CHART 1

Chart 1
☐ Sea Green 4186 (sleeve and body), Dark Violet 448 (yoke)

● Lavender 4088 (sleeve and body), Hot Pink 4686(yoke)

Chart 3
☐ Sea Green 4186
● Violet 448
○ Cyclamen 4886

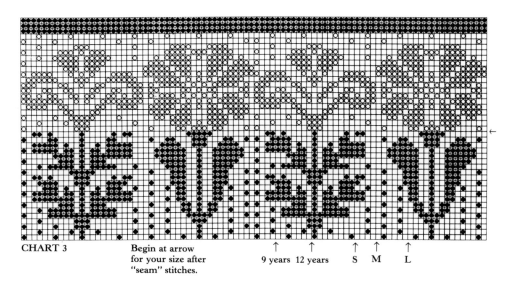

CHART 3   Begin at arrow for your size after "seam" stitches.

↑   ↑   ↑ ↑ ↑
9 years 12 years   S   M   L

Chart 2
□ Light Blue 4385
● Midnight Blue 467

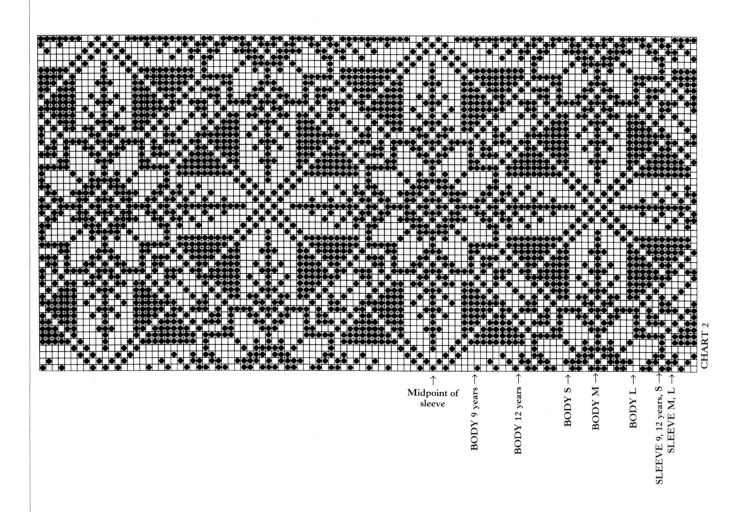

↑
Midpoint of
sleeve

BODY 9 years →

BODY 12 years →

BODY S →

BODY M →

BODY L →

SLEEVE 9, 12 years, S →
SLEEVE M, L →

CHART 2

DESIGN 11

FLOWERING RAGLAN PULLOVER

Chart 1
□ Medium Green 458
● Cyclamen 4886

Chart 2
□ Light Green 493/Sea Green 4186
● Red 424/Hot Pink 4686

Chart 3
□ Light Green 493
● Dark Violet 448

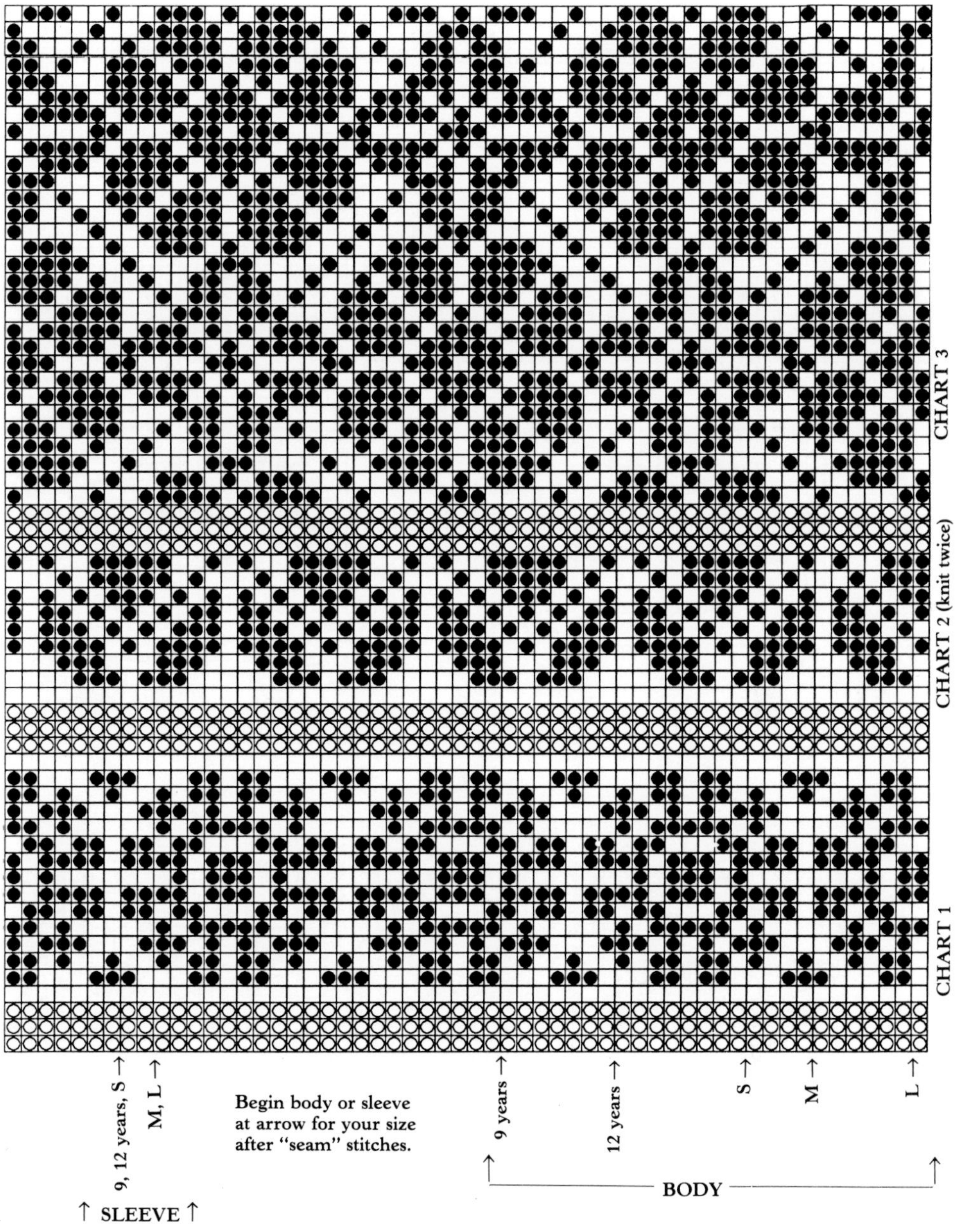

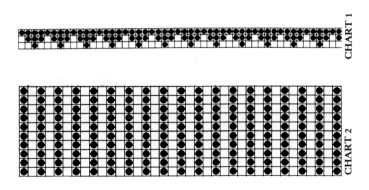

CHART 3
CHART 2 (knit twice)
CHART 1
9, 12 years, S →
M, L →
Begin body or sleeve at arrow for your size after "seam" stitches.
9 years →
12 years →
S →
M →
L →
↑ SLEEVE ↑
BODY

DESIGN 12

BIRDS ON A FENCE PULLOVER

CHART 1

CHART 2

Chart 1
□ Charcoal 1387
● Orange 157

Chart 2
□ Charcoal 1387
● Cyclamen 173

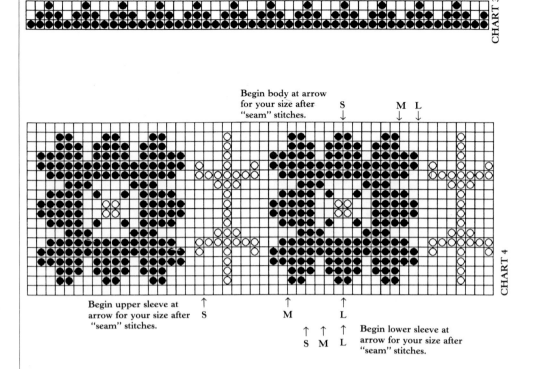

Chart 3
☐ Charcoal 1387
● Orange 157

Chart 4
☐ Charcoal 1387
● Cyclamen 173
○ Yellow Green 198

Chart 5
☐ Yellow Green 198
● Charcoal 1387

CHART 3

Begin body at arrow
for your size after
"seam" stitches.

S
↓

M   L
↓   ↓

Begin upper sleeve at
arrow for your size after
"seam" stitches.

S ↑

M ↑

L ↑

S ↑   M ↑   L ↑

Begin lower sleeve at
arrow for your size after
"seam" stitches.

CHART 4

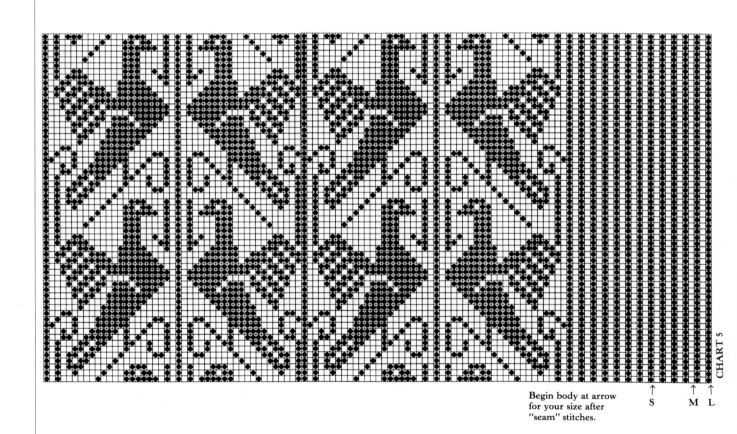

Begin body at arrow
for your size after
"seam" stitches.

S ↑   M ↑   L ↑

CHART 5

CHARCOAL AND HOT PINK JACKET

Begin here for
lower sleeve ↓

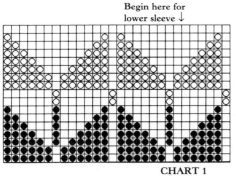

CHART 1

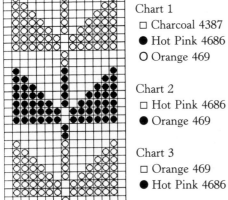

CHART 4

Chart 1
□ Charcoal 4387
● Hot Pink 4686
○ Orange 469

Chart 2
□ Hot Pink 4686
● Orange 469

Chart 3
□ Orange 469
● Hot Pink 4686

Chart 4
□ Charcoal 4387
● Hot Pink 4686
○ Orange 469

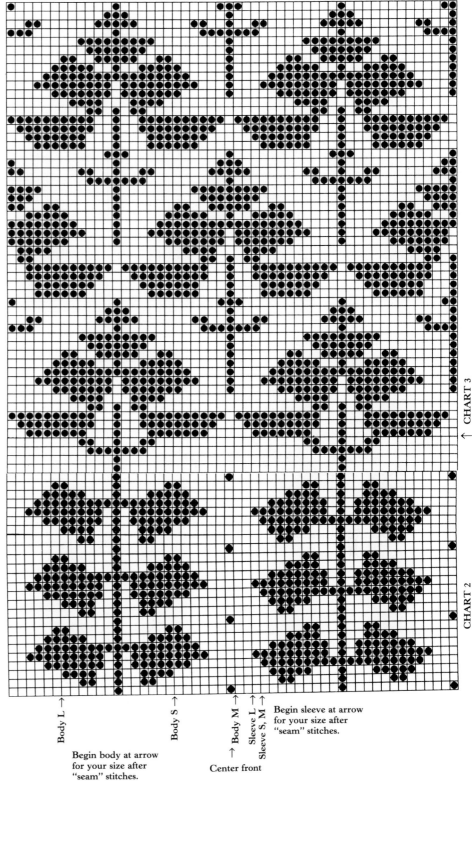

CHART 3

← CHART 2

Body L →

Body S →

→ Body M

Sleeve L →

Sleeve S, M →

Begin sleeve at arrow
for your size after
"seam" stitches.

Begin body at arrow
for your size after
"seam" stitches.

Center front

DESIGN 14

A LITTLE JUMPSUIT

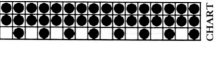

CHART 3

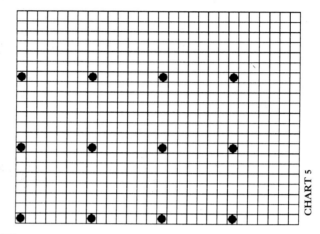

CHART 5

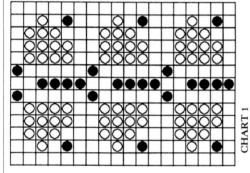

CHART 1

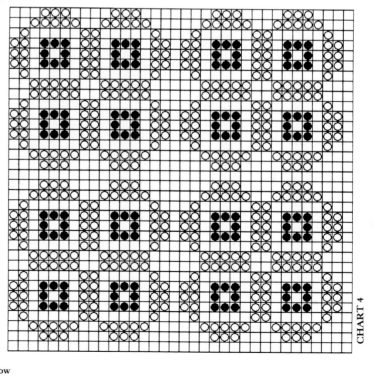

CHART 4

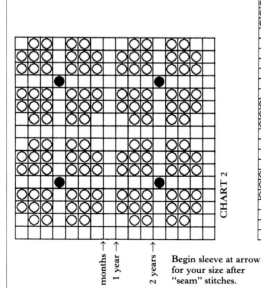

CHART 2

Chart 1
□ Light Pink B79
● Black B36
○ Yellow B20

Chart 1
□ Light Pink B79 (legs),
  Dark Pink (sleeves)
● Black B36
○ Dark Pink B45 (legs),
  Light Pink B79 (sleeves)

Chart 3
□ Light Pink B79 (legs),
  Dark Pink B45 (sleeves)
● Black B36

Chart 4
□ Dark Pink B45
● Black B36
○ Yellow B20

Chart 5
□ Yellow B20
● Dark Pink B45

6 months →
1 year →
2 years →

**Begin sleeve at arrow
for your size after
"seam" stitches.**

TONE'S
SILVER
BROOCH
PULLOVER

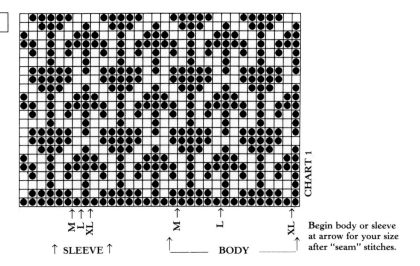

CHART 1

↑↑↑   ↑   ↑   ↑
M L XL   M   L   XL

↑ SLEEVE ↑   ⌊_____ BODY _____⌋

Begin body or sleeve
at arrow for your size
after "seam" stitches.

Chart 1
□ Gray Blue 168
  (sleeve and back of body)

● Charcoal 107
  (sleeve and back of body)

Chart 2
□ Gray Blue 168 (front of body)
● Charcoal 107 (front of body)

CHART 2

Begin body at arrow
for your size after
"seam" stitches.

M   L   XL

NAVY ON PASTEL FOR A SMALL CHILD

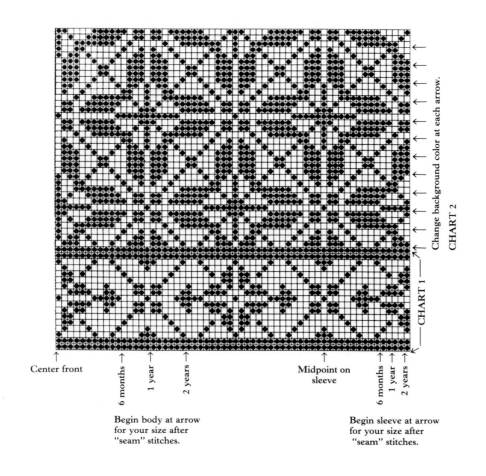

Change background color at each arrow.

CHART 2

CHART 1

Center front

6 months

1 year

2 years

Begin body at arrow for your size after "seam" stitches.

Midpoint on sleeve

6 months

1 year

2 years

Begin sleeve at arrow for your size after "seam" stitches.

Chart 1
☐ Medium Blue B51
● Navy Blue B59

Chart 2
☐ Light Blue B72/Lilac B96/
   Light Blue B72/Turquoise B76

● Navy Blue B59

DESIGN 17

SKI SWEATERS FOR THE WHOLE FAMILY

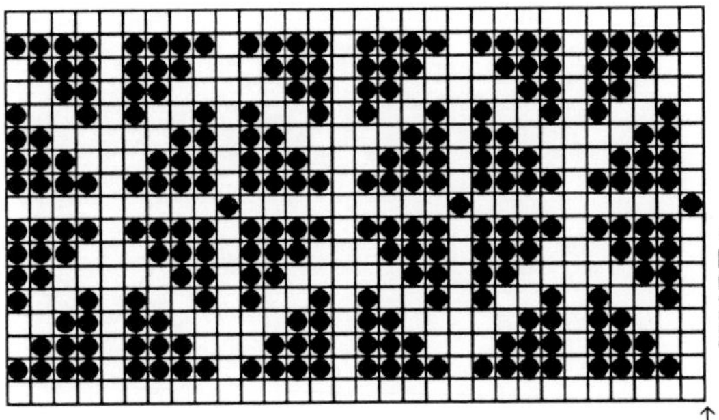

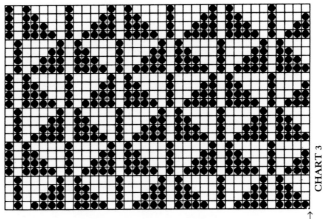

CHART 1
Begin here for all sizes.

CHART 2
Begin here for all sizes.

CHART 3
Begin here for all sizes.

Chart 1
□ Light Gray 404
● Charcoal 414

Chart 2
□ Light Gray 404
● Charcoal 414

Chart 3
□ Light Gray 404
● Charcoal 414

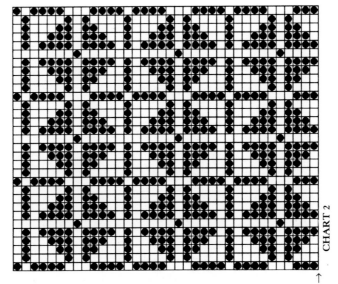

BANDED PULLOVER

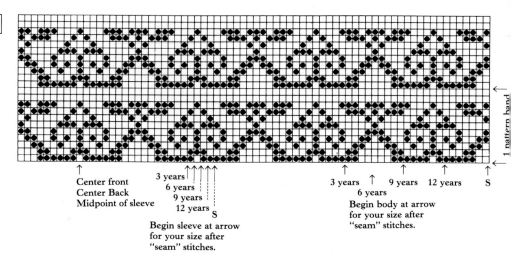

1 pattern band

↑
Center front
Center Back
Midpoint of sleeve

3 years
6 years
9 years
12 years
S

Begin sleeve at arrow for your size after "seam" stitches.

3 years   9 years   12 years
6 years   S

Begin body at arrow for your size after "seam" stitches.

The same band of pattern is repeated with these colors:

□ Red 144	Gray Blue 151	Medium Brown 164	Gray Blue 151 (body only)	Red 144 (body only)	Deep Violet 112
● Deep Violet 112	Deep Violet 112	Gray Blue 151	Deep Violet 112 (body only)	Deep Violet 112 (body only)	Red 144

SANDAL-WOOD AND BLACK PULLOVER

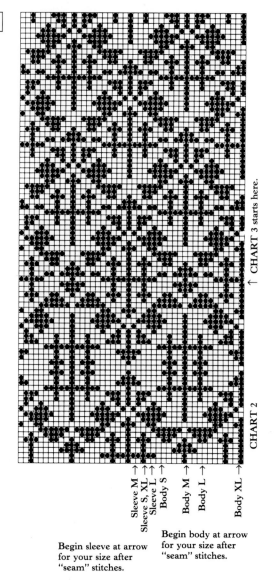

← CHART 3 starts here.

CHART 2

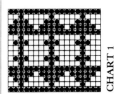

CHART 1

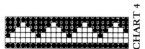

CHART 4

Sleeve M →
Sleeve S, XL →
Sleeve L →
Body S →
Body M →
Body L →
Body XL →

Begin sleeve at arrow for your size after "seam" stitches.

Begin body at arrow for your size after "seam" stitches.

Chart 1
□ Sandalwood 140
● Black 136

Chart 2
□ Sandalwood 140
● Black 136

Chart 3
□ Sandalwood 140
● Black 136

Chart 4
□ Sandalwood 140
● Black 136

GEOMETRIC LIGHTS PULLOVER

Chart 1
□ Sheep's Brown 111
O Purple 112

Chart 2
□ Sheep's Brown 111
● Purple 112
O Yellow 146/Cinnamon 181
   Burgundy 128/Black 136

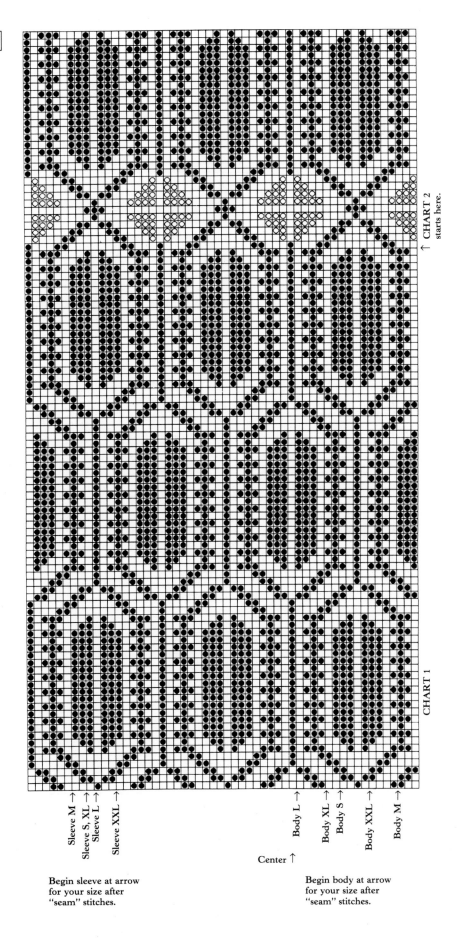

↑ CHART 2 starts here.

CHART 1

Sleeve M →
Sleeve S, XL →
Sleeve L →
Sleeve XXL →

Body L →
Body XL →
Body S →
Body XXL →
Body M →

Center ↑

Begin sleeve at arrow
for your size after
"seam" stitches.

Begin body at arrow
for your size after
"seam" stitches.

DOUBLE-BREASTED JACKET

Chart 1
□ Gray Blue 451
● Brown 464

Chart 2
□ Brown 464
● Lavender 4088
○ Gray Blue 451/Baby Blue 4385

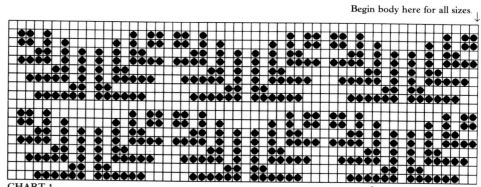

Begin body here for all sizes. ↓

CHART 1

↑ Begin sleeve here
for all sizes.

↑ ↑ ↑ Begin sleeve at arrow
XL L XXL for your size after
"seam" stitches.

↑ Begin body here for all sizes.

CHART 2

DESIGN 22

TAILORED JACKET WITH SADDLE SHOULDERS

Chart 1
● Grape 442
□ Cinnamon 425

Chart 3
○ Cinnamon 425
⊠ Gold 431

Chart 4
○ Rose 465
⊡ Orange 461
● Grape 442

Chart 5
□ Cinnamon 425
● Grape 442

Chart 6
● Rose 465
□ Cinnamon 425

Chart 7
● Grape 442
⊡ Orange 461
○ Rose 465

Chart 8
□ Cinnamon 425
⊠ Gold 431

Chart 9
□ Cinnamon 425
● Grape 442

Chart 10
□ Cinnamon 425
● Grape 442

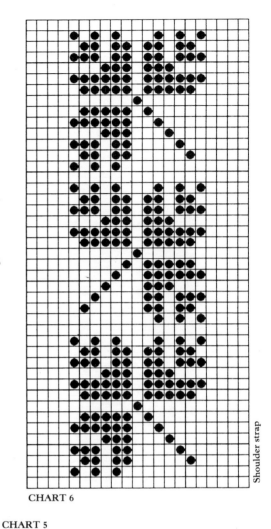

Shoulder strap

CHART 6

CHART 5

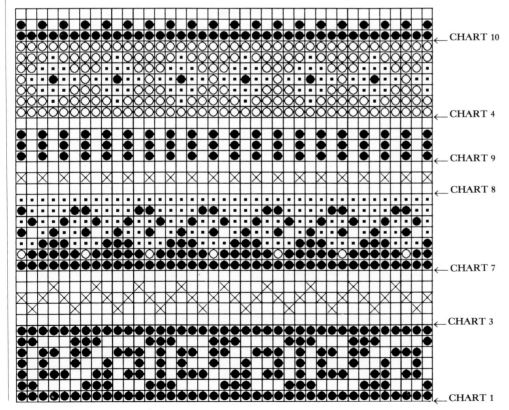

← **CHART 10**

← **CHART 4**

← **CHART 9**

← **CHART 8**

← **CHART 7**

← **CHART 3**

← **CHART 1**

Chart 2

□ Rose 465 (body),
   Cinnamon 425 (sleeve)

● Cinnamon 425 (body),
   Rose 465 (sleeve)

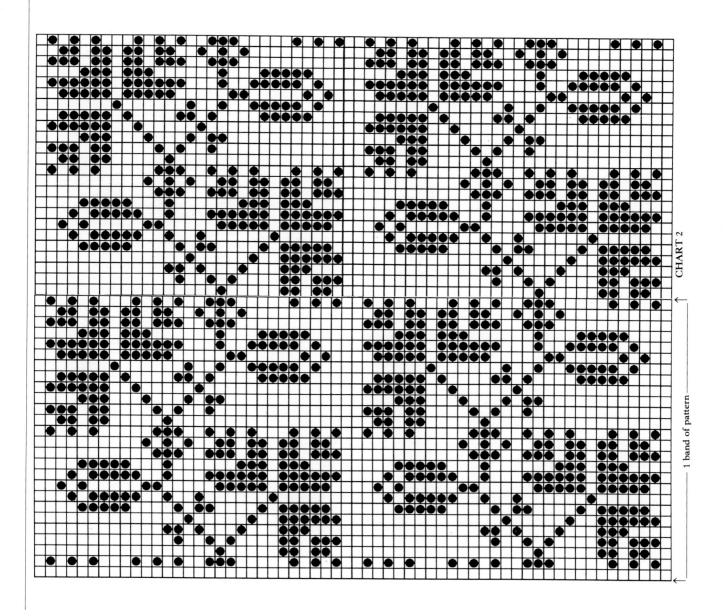

CHART 2

1 band of pattern

BOLERO

Chart 1
- □ Medium Violet 470
- ● Light Rust 434
  Medium Rust 419
  Dark Rust 428

Chart 3
- □ Medium Violet 470
- ● Dark Rust 428
  Medium Rust 419
  Light Rust 434

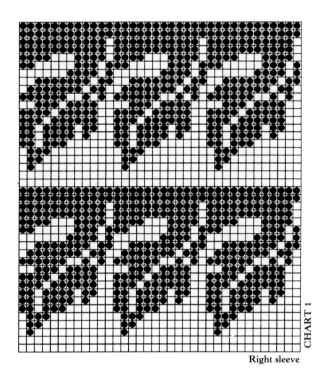

CHART 1

Right sleeve

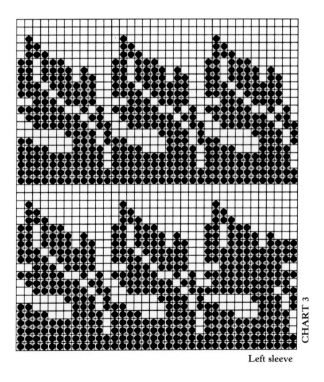

CHART 3

Left sleeve

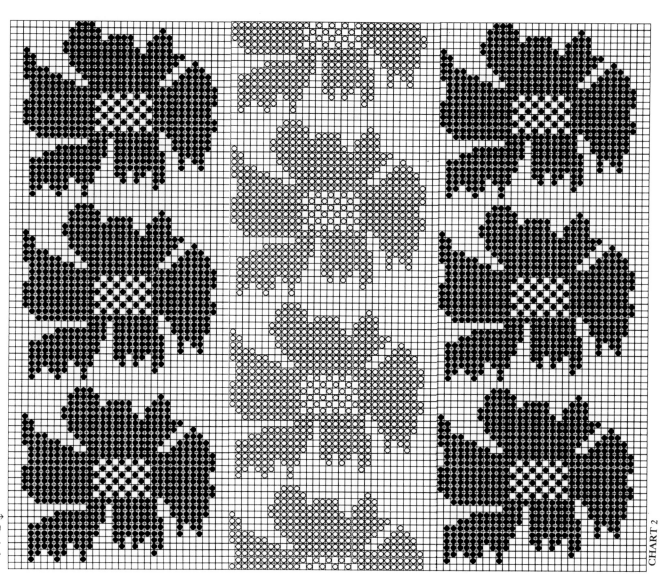

→ Begin here and work the chart sideways.

CHART 2

Chart 2
□ Charcoal 4387
● Light Burgundy 499
  Red Wine 497
  Light Burgundy 499

MAN'S
JACKET
WITH
GEOMETRICS

Chart 1
□ Antique Gold 417
● Burgundy 480

Chart 2
□ Antique Gold 417
● Burgundy 480

CHART 2

Begin at arrow for all sizes ↑
after the "seam" stitches.

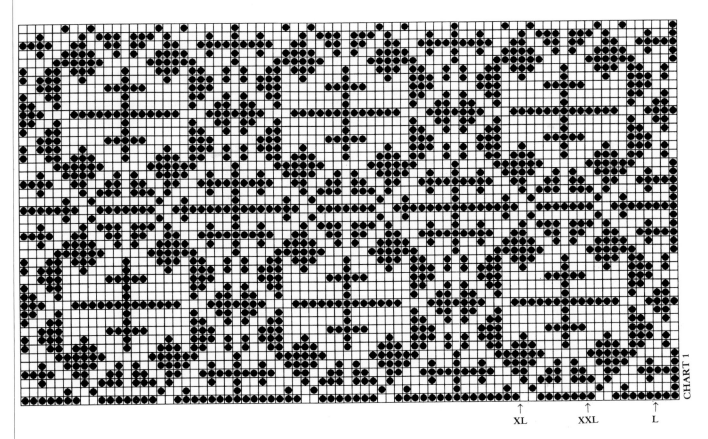

CHART 1

XL   XXL   L

Begin body at arrow for
your size after "seam" stitches.

THE BIG, BIG TRIANGLE

Chart 1
☐ Dusky Rose 490
● Antique Gold 417
○ Wooden Rose 440

Detail of increase at the back point.

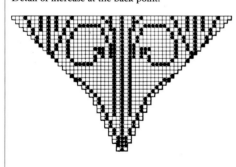

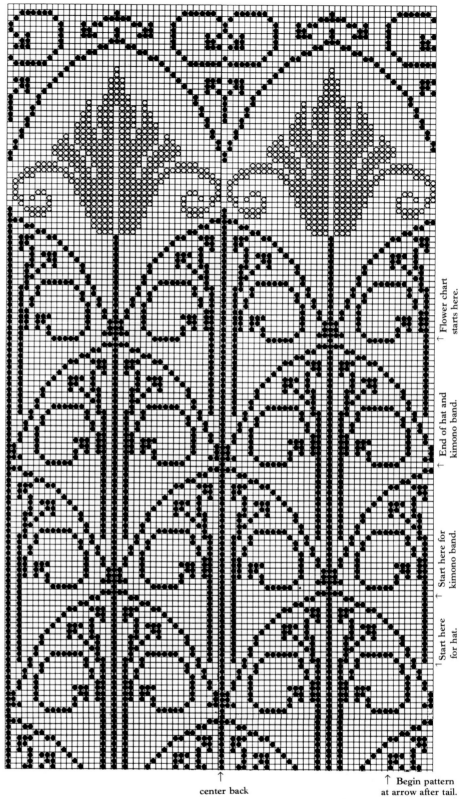

↑ Flower chart starts here.

↑ End of hat and kimono band.

↑ Start here for kimono band.

↑ Start here for hat.

↑
center back

↑ Begin pattern at arrow after tail.

DESIGN 26

NORDIC CARVING SWEATER

Chart 1	Chart 2	Chart 3	or	Chart 4
□ Blue 438	□ Black 436	□ Black 436	● Dark Rust 428	□ Black 436
● Black 436	● Light Rust 434	● Cinnamon 425		● Blue 438
		O Light Rust 434	O Yellow Green 498	

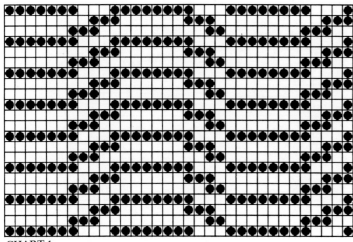

CHART 1

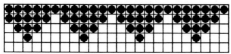

CHART 2

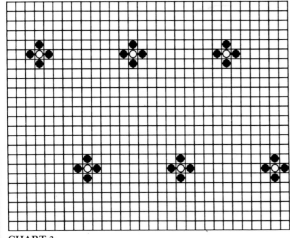

CHART 3

Begin body at arrow for your size.

S →
M →
L →

Begin cap here. →

CHART 4

A DEAR LITTLE DRESS

Chart 1
● Lavender 4088
□ Yellow Green 498

Chart 2
□ Red Violet 496
● Light Rust 434
○ Yellow Green 498
⊠ Deep Violet 474

Chart 3
□ Lavender 4088
● Red Violet 496
○ Yellow Green 498

or

● Deep Violet 474
○ Light Rust 434

CHART 3

Begin at arrow for ↑
all sizes after
"seam" stitches.

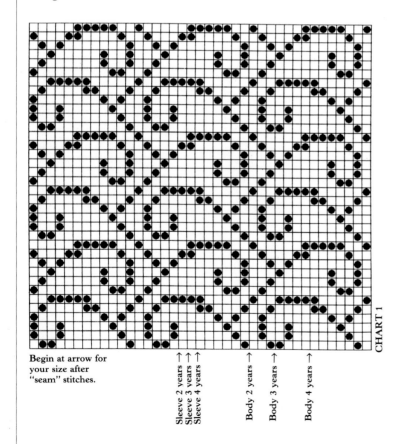

CHART 1

Begin at arrow for
your size after
"seam" stitches.

Sleeve 2 years → ↑
Sleeve 3 years → ↑
Sleeve 4 years → ↑

Body 2 years →

Body 3 years →

Body 4 years →

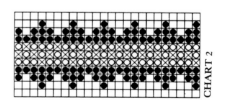

CHART 2

THE SWEATER CAPE

Chart 1
□ Light Burgundy 499
● Black 436
○ Light Rust 434

Chart 2
□ Light Burgundy 499
● Black 436
○ Light Rust 434

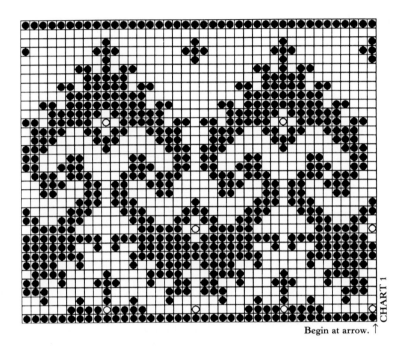

CHART 1

Begin at arrow. ↑

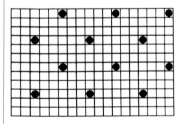

CHART 2

Begin at arrow. ↑

INDEX

BOOKS OF RELATED INTEREST

Gibson-Roberts, Priscilla A. *Knitting in the Old Way.* Loveland, CO: Interweave, 1985.

Lind, Vibeke. *Knitting in the Nordic Tradition.* Asheville, NC: Lark Books, 1985.

McGregor, Sheila. *The Complete Book of Traditional Scandinavian Knitting.* New York: St. Martin, 1984.

Pagoldh, Susanne. *Nordic Knitting: Thirty-One Patterns in the Scandinavian Tradition.* Loveland, CO: Interweave, 1991.

Starmore, Alice. *Scandinavian Knitwear.* New York: Van Nostrand Reinhold, 1982.

Thomas, Mary. *Mary Thomas's Knitting Book.* New York: Dover, 1972.

U.S. SUPPLIERS OF RAUMA YARNS

East

Charlotte's Web
137 Epping Road
Exeter, NH 03833
(603) 778-1417
   Strikkegarn and Finullgarn, retail.

Nordic Fiber Arts
4 Cutts Road
Durham, NH 03824
(603) 868-1196
   Strikkegarn and Finullgarn, wholesale and retail.

The Spinning Wheel
2 Ridge Street
Dover, NH 03820
(603) 749-4246
   Strikkegarn, retail.

The Whippletree, Inc.
7 Central Street
Woodstock, VT 05091
(802) 457-1325
   Strikkegarn, retail.

The Yarn Basket
18 Ladd Street
Portsmouth, NH 03801
(603) 431-9301
   Strikkegarn, retail.

Central

Norsk Engros U.S.A., Inc.
P.O. Box 229
Decorah, IA 52101
(800) 553-0014
   Wholesale only: write or phone for the address of the retail supplier nearest you.

Ram Wools
400 First Avenue
Minneapolis, MN 55401
(612) 339-4993
   Strikkegarn, retail.

West

The Unique
11 E. Bijou
Colorado Springs, CO 80903
(719) 473-9406
   Strikkegarn, Finullgarn, and Vamsegarn, retail.